Fun & Easy Games

Group

Loveland, Colorado

Fun & Easy Games

Copyright © 1998

Credits

Contributing Authors: Jody Brolsma, Mikal Keefer, Ken and Susan Kellner, Karl and Gina Leuthauser, Julie Meiklejohn, Amy Nappa, Amy Simpson, Beth Rowland Wolf, and Paul Woods
Editor: Jan Kershner
Creative Development Editor: Dave Thornton
Chief Creative Officer: Joani Schultz
Copy Editor: Helen Turnbull
Art Director: Ray Tollison
Cover Art Director: Jeff A. Storm
Computer Graphic Artist: Randy Kady
Cover Designer: Liz Howe
Illustrator: Liz Howe
Production Manager: Peggy Naylor

Library of Congress Cataloging-in-Publication Data
Fun & easy games : [contributing authors, Jody Brolsma ... et al.
    editor, Jan Kershner].
        p. cm.
    ISBN 0-7644-2042-9
    1. Games in Christian education. 2. Church work with children.
I. Brolsma, Jody. II. Kershner, Jan
BV1536.3.F84 1998
268'.432—dc21   97-35295
                                                                            CIP

10 9 8 7 6 5 4 3 2 1   07 06 05 04 03 02 01 00 99 98
Printed in the United States of America.

268
F

5/40

Contents —

Large Indoor-Space Games   33

Outdoor Games   56

Introduction

Child's play. How important is it?

Play is an integral part of childhood. And it's an integral part of ministry, too. As children play together, they're not only having fun, they're learning valuable Christian skills as well. Patience, respect, and cooperation can all be learned on the playing field.

That's the best-case scenario. But too often, play can have a negative impact on kids. They learn that they're not fast enough, tall enough, or coordinated enough. They learn that they're not wanted or that they're not "good enough."

That's why this book is so important. *Fun & Easy Games* is a book about positive play. Everyone plays. Everyone cooperates. And no one feels like a loser!

With so many games to choose from, you'll never be at a loss for a quick and easy game to add to your children's ministry program. Help your kids get to know each other, lead into a lesson, make a point, or just have fun! There are games for the classroom, games to play outside, games that are perfect for large indoor spaces, and travel games to make your trips more enjoyable.

But that's not all. Every game in *Fun & Easy Games* is designed to foster cooperation. Kids play *with* each other, not *against* each other. So everyone's a winner!

As they play the games in this book, kids will be learning how to have fun together without the put-downs that competition so often produces. Kids will grow in their faith as they see that cooperation, not competition, creates a servant's heart.

And the games are so easy! Each game contains a quick overview that tells you what age level the game works best with, and what energy level the game requires. So choose a high-energy game to get the wiggles out, or a low-energy game to lead into your devotion. (The handy energy-level index makes the book especially user-friendly!)

Remember: It's only child's play, but it can have a permanent impact. So add a little fun to your ministry—the noncompetitive way!

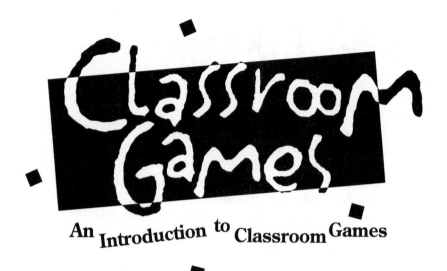

An Introduction to Classroom Games

Make your classroom a place kids want to be!

Choose from the classroom games on the following pages to add excitement and fun to your time together. Your kids will love the entertainment and challenge these games afford. And you'll love how easy and low-prep the games are. Everyone will love the noncompetitive, affirming nature of these classroom games.

Most of the games are low- or medium-energy, so they can be played easily and safely in your classroom setting. Use the games as quick lead-ins to lessons, as transitions between activities, or any time you just want to have some fun!

Noah's Ark ━━━━

Best For: Kindergarten through third grade
Energy Level: Low
Supplies: Slips of paper, a pen or pencil, and a basket or bowl

The Fun:

This is a fun game in itself, but it also doubles as a great transition between activities or as a way to have kids form new groups.

Before the game, write the name of an animal on each slip of paper. Be sure you have one slip of paper for each child. Write the name of each animal on several slips, based on the number in each group you want to form. For example, if you want to form groups of three, write "lion" (or the name of another animal) on three slips of paper.

Place the slips of paper in a bowl or basket, and instruct each child to choose a paper slip. Have children read their slips of paper without letting anyone else see them.

 If most of the children in your class are non-readers, draw simple pictures or use animal stickers on the paper slips.

When each child has read a slip of paper, instruct children to begin making animal noises that correspond to their assigned animals. Their task is to listen to the noises the other children are making, and find those children who have been assigned the same animals.

For extra fun, have young children act out the animals' motions as well. Offer older children more of a challenge by having them silently act out the animals, or have children keep their eyes closed as they search for the other "animals" in their groups. (Make sure to remove any obstacles in the room that could pose a tripping hazard.)

When children find their corresponding "animals," have animals sit together in groups. When everyone is sitting in a group, have children in each group work together to write a song or cheer describing their animal. For example, children might think of a cheer such as the following:

One, two, three, four!
We're the lions, hear us roar!

Circulate among groups to offer help as needed. If children can't think of a cheer or song, suggest the tunes of familiar songs, such as "Row, Row, Row Your Boat," or "Frère Jacques." When all the groups are ready, have groups take turns presenting their cheers or songs and introducing their animals to each other.

¤Game Guide

It's easy to tie this game to familiar Bible stories. The story of Noah's ark is a natural, as are the story of Daniel and the lion's den and any of the stories using birds, sheep, or donkeys.

Fun formations ━━━━

Best For: Second through sixth grade
Energy Level: Medium
Supplies: None

The fun:

Playing this game is a great way to help kids remember what they're learning!

Move chairs, tables, and other furniture to the edges of the room. Have kids form groups of four, and have groups space themselves about the room. Call out a letter of the alphabet. Instruct kids to work together in their groups—as quickly as possible—to stand in the shape of that letter.

Then call out another letter, and have them form the shape of that letter. Time kids' efforts, and encourage them to try to improve their time with each letter.

For variety, try asking kids to form geometric shapes, animals, or even words! Older kids may enjoy the challenge of forming answers to Bible questions.

Sticker Bingo ━━━━

Best For: Kindergarten through third grade
Energy Level: Low
Supplies: Assorted stickers (enough for each child to give one
sticker to each other child), paper, and a pen

The Fun:

Use this game to remind your kids that each one of them is important to the group!

Before the game, use a pen to draw a Bingo grid on a sheet of paper. Create one square for each child who might possibly be present for the game. Make one photocopy of the grid for each child.

 **Game Guide** If you have a large group of children, you may want to divide them into two or more smaller groups to play this game.

Give each child a Bingo grid and enough stickers so he or she may give away a sticker to every other participant. Instruct kids to move as quickly as they can, walking around the room and collecting one sticker from each of the other children in the room. As they collect their stickers, have them place each sticker on a separate square of the Bingo grid.

The game is over when each child has filled his or her Bingo grid. You may want to use this opportunity to discuss with children that each of them is important to the group. Just as the Bingo grid wasn't complete without a sticker from every child in your class, explain that your group just isn't complete without each member.

Have them look at their bright, fun collections of stickers and realize that the "collection" of children would not be complete without any one child.

¤ Game Guide

If you've anticipated the attendance of more children than actually play the game, instruct kids to cross out any extra squares on their Bingo grids.

Character Questions ⟶

Best For: Second through fourth grade
Energy Level: Low
Supplies: Pictures of cartoon characters or other well-known characters and tape

The Fun:

This game will have kids guessing at their own identities!

Tape a picture of a cartoon character or other well-known character to the back of each child. As you do so, be sure children don't see the pictures you're taping to their backs.

Instruct children to walk around the room, asking yes-or-no questions of each other, trying to guess the identity of the characters taped to their backs. They may ask *only* yes-or-no questions, and they can ask each person only one question.

For example, a child may ask another child, "Am I a cartoon animal?" That child will answer "yes" or "no," and then the child who asked the question must move on to another child for his or her next question.

When children think they know the identities of their characters, they may tell their guesses to you or another adult. If they're incorrect, they should stay in the game, continuing to ask questions. If they're correct, they should continue to answer questions for other children.

Be sure children realize they must be truthful in answering one another's questions.

¤ Game Guide

Children's coloring books are good sources for pictures of cartoon characters and other well-known characters.

Penny Elbow ━━━

Best For: Fifth and sixth grade
Energy Level: Low
Supplies: Three pennies for each child

The Fun:

This is a game for the truly sophisticated and quick of hand. Show kids how you stack up to three pennies on your elbow, then with a quick downward motion, catch them in the hand of the same arm.

Here's how it's done:

1. Roll up your sleeves so your elbow is unencumbered.

2. Bend your elbow so it's sticking straight out ahead of you, and your hand is almost palm up.

3. On your elbow, stack several pennies. (You might want to begin with just one penny to start.)

4. Quickly flick your arm down and scoop the pennies with your hand.

You must move quickly. The pennies will "hang" in the air for a split second—then fall. Your job is to get your hand over them before they fall.

Once your kids have the hang of it, increase the number of pennies in their stacks.

Stuck on You ━━━━

Best For: Kindergarten through fourth grade
Energy Level: Medium
Supplies: About five inflated balloons per child, and one paper
grocery sack for every five children

The Fun:

Before the game, fill several paper grocery sacks with inflated balloons. Form groups of five, then give each group a sack of balloons. Have each group stand in a circle. Instruct each group to choose one person to be a Balloon Buddy.

Tell kids that in this game, each group will try to cover its Balloon Buddy with balloons. Explain that when you say "go," kids should start rubbing balloons on their heads to get the balloons good and sticky with static! Then they can stick the balloons to their Balloon Buddy. When the Buddy is covered, he or she will try to walk around the circle without losing any balloons. Then the Balloon Buddy will choose another person to be the Buddy.

Give the starting signal and let the fun begin! When everyone has had a turn to be a Balloon Buddy, have groups return their balloons to their paper sacks. Then gather kids in a large circle. Place all the bags of balloons in the middle of the circle.

Then tell kids they'll have thirty seconds to stick balloons to others in the circle, while trying to keep others from sticking balloons on them! Explain that once a balloon is stuck to a child, the child can't take it off.

After thirty seconds, have kids each count the number of balloons stuck to them. Have the kids play again; then have kids pop their balloons.

Ping-Pong Popcorn ━━━━

Best For: All ages
Energy Level: Medium
Supplies: Masking tape, pencils, and one plastic spoon and a Ping-Pong ball per child (If you can't purchase Ping-Pong

balls, have kids write their names on strips of masking tape and attach a tape strip to a cotton ball for each child.)

The Fun:

Before the game, divide your playing area in half by placing a masking tape strip across the middle of the floor. Distribute pencils and Ping-Pong balls and have each child write his or her name on a ball. Form two groups and have groups move to opposite sides of the playing area and sit so they're facing the other group.

Give each child a plastic spoon. Tell kids when you give the signal, they can use their spoons to launch the Ping-Pong balls across the room. Then kids can continue launching other Ping-Pong balls that come their way back to the other side of the room.

Caution kids to be careful not to hurt others as they launch their Ping-Pong balls, and to remain in place throughout the game. Explain that when you call time, kids should each grab the closest Ping-Pong ball and hold onto it.

Let kids launch the Ping-Pong balls, and continue play for thirty seconds. Call time and wait for everyone to grab a Ping-Pong ball. Then tell kids to quickly find the person whose name is on the ball they're holding. Kids should then tell that person their favorite flavor of ice cream. Allow a minute for kids to find each other and trade information; then have them return to their groups.

Have the kids play again, but change the information kids must exchange. You might have children tell their least favorite vegetable, the last movie they saw, a favorite vacation spot, or a joke they heard recently.

Quick Change

Best For: First through third grade
Energy Level: Medium
Supplies: Oversized dress-up clothes, gift wrap, tape, boxes, treats, a shoe box, and one pair of dice

The Fun:

Before the game, gift-wrap a bag of treats in a small box. Place the box inside a larger box and gift-wrap it again. Continue until you've gift-wrapped the treats four times.

Form a circle and place the clothing and gift box in the middle of the circle. Place the dice in the bottom half of a shoe box. Explain that you'll pass this box around and kids can take turns rolling the dice in it.

If a child rolls doubles, he or she should pass the box and run to the middle of the circle. Then the child will put all the dress-up clothes on, then unwrap the present. Meanwhile, kids will keep passing the box and rolling the dice. If someone else rolls doubles, that person will come to the middle of the circle. The first child will remove the dress-up clothes, give them to the second child to put on, then return to his or her seat.

Tell kids that when someone unwraps the final box and finds what's inside, everyone will share it.

When someone finally reaches the treats, have that person share them with the class. If you have more than ten children, pass two pairs of dice to allow more children to have a turn.

Action!

Best For: Third through sixth grade
Energy Level: Medium
Supplies: None

The Fun:

In this game, kids will think they're just having fun, but will actually be cultivating their creativity!

Have kids form small groups, and have each group form a line. Tell the first person in each line that he or she should act out an event without saying a word. Encourage children to try to act out familiar things that others will recognize. For example, kids can pretend they're playing baseball, cooking pancakes, or riding on a horse.

After kids begin, call time and tell the actors to freeze exactly where they are. Explain that the next child in line is to take the first actor's place by assuming the exact position that person is in. The new actor should then begin acting out a different event starting from the position the first actor was in.

For example, if the first actor was pretending to swing a baseball bat and froze while holding the bat on his or her shoulder, the second actor could take the first actor's place and pretend to carry a sack on his or her shoulder then set the sack on the ground. Continue the game until everyone has had a chance to act out an event.

Odd Toss Out

Best For: Third through sixth grade
Energy Level: Low
Supplies: Eight pennies for each child

The Fun:

Form trios. Give each child exactly eight pennies. Demonstrate how to flip a penny; then give kids a chance to practice.

¤ Game Guide

The skill of penny flipping can't be adequately described in print; it must be learned from an experienced flipper. If you don't know how to flip a coin, recruit someone who knows. They'll be honored you asked, as flippers seldom get to strut their stuff.

Actually, flipping coins isn't essential. Kids can simply shake coins in their cupped hands and then drop coins on the floor.

In each trio, have each child shake or flip one coin, letting it land on the floor. If all three pennies are "heads" or "tails," kids will retrieve their coins and play again. If there's a mixture of heads and tails, whoever has the coin that is the "odd man out" (the coin that's heads when there are two tails, or the coin that's tails when there are two heads) will pick up all three coins.

The goal of the game is to collect as many coins as possible. But because it's a game of chance, all three players have an equal opportunity to win.

In theory, given enough time, all kids will eventually again have eight coins. That's what statistics say...but it never happens. So put a time limit on the game (ninety seconds is about right) and have kids count their coins when you call time.

Drawing in the Dark

Best For: Third through sixth grade
Energy Level: Low
Supplies: Newsprint, markers, tape, and towels

The Fun:

This is a great game to use to help kids understand how we need Jesus' light in our lives.

If your regular meeting room has windows, trade rooms with another class for the day. If that's not feasible, cover your windows with black plastic trash bags or sheets. Use towels to prevent light from coming through under your door. The room needs to be as dark as possible.

Tape one sheet of newsprint to a wall for every four children in your group. Make certain you tape the sheets of newsprint low enough for your kids to draw on. Set markers near each of the newsprint sheets.

Form groups of four and direct the groups to each gather around a sheet of newsprint. Have each group use a marker to divide its newsprint into four sections. Ask a volunteer from each group to get in a huddle with you. Instruct the volunteers to draw a simple picture of a tree on one of the four sections of the newsprint when you say to begin. Remind them not to tell others what they are drawing. Have the volunteers return to their groups.

Tell children that the volunteers will draw a picture and the other team members must try to figure out what the volunteers have drawn. Inform the volunteers they'll have forty-five seconds to draw their pictures—in the dark!

Have the volunteers put the markers in the middle of one of the sections. Turn off the lights, and have the volunteers begin drawing. After forty-five seconds, turn the lights back on and allow thirty seconds for kids to guess what the drawing represents.

Repeat the above instructions so all four kids in every group have an opportunity to draw. Suggest simple pictures such as a cross, a rainbow, or a heart. Older kids will enjoy the challenge of drawing pictures pertaining to the Bible story you're studying.

Skyscraper ━━━

Best For: Third through sixth grade
Energy Level: Medium
Supplies: Masking tape and paper

The Fun:

This game can be used to help form group identity or just to help kids get to know each other better. It can also be used to introduce the story of the Tower of Babel (Genesis 11:1-9).

Have kids form groups of three. (If you have a large number of kids, just make your groups larger.) Give each group a stack of paper and masking tape. Instruct each group to build a tower using the paper and tape. Encourage groups to make the towers as high as possible.

If children aren't certain how to build the towers, show them how to make "blocks" by rolling pieces of paper into cylinders or folding them in half to make tents.

For younger children, use books or hymnals instead of paper for building materials. Try to let kids do as much of the work on their own as possible. If children have difficulty building the towers, show them how to construct a wide base to make a pyramid-like building.

To challenge older kids, have them create the paper towers without using tape.

Give kids five minutes to build the towers as high as possible. Have groups admire each other's towers, and congratulate the builders. Recycle the paper when your meeting is over.

Special Strengths ━━━

Best For: Third through sixth grade
Energy Level: Medium
Supplies: Index cards and markers

The Fun:

Use this game to build up the members of your group as kids discover what makes each of them so special.

Have kids form groups of three to five. Give each group

twelve to twenty index cards and at least as many markers as there are members of the group. Have children divide the index cards evenly among the group's members.

Explain that it will be each group's job to build a "house of strengths." Tell kids to interview the other members of the group to find out what makes them so special. Kids might ask each other questions about favorite sports, musical talents, interests and hobbies, or favorite foods. Tell kids to make sure each person in the group has a chance to be interviewed.

Then have kids write or draw one of the special qualities they've discovered on each index card. Tell kids to write on the other side of the card the name of the person who possesses the quality. Circulate among the groups to offer help and encouragement.

When the kids finish writing on all the cards, give them ten minutes to build a house with their index cards.

After ten minutes, call time and have groups stop building. Let groups admire each other's building talents. Then, let groups take turns dismantling their houses by taking off the cards one by one and reading the special qualities and names aloud to the rest of the class.

Double Time! ━━━

Best For: All ages
Energy Level: High
Supplies: None

The Fun:

Here's a fun way to burn off kids' surplus energy and review the life story of a Bible hero at the same time! You might want to use this game when you're studying Acts 8:1-3, 9:1-9; and 2 Corinthians 11:23-30. Or use it any time as a quick, fun Bible review.

Before the game, ask children if they know what the fast-forward button is for on their VCRs at home. Although most kids will be familiar with the concept of fast-forward motion, make sure all of your children understand the term.

Then tell kids they'll be acting out the Apostle Paul's life—*on fast-forward*. What took Paul years to do they'll whip through in just minutes!

Arrange kids in circles of no more than fourteen students,

and have them stand at least an arm's length from each other. Explain that although they'll be moving quickly, they'll remain in place. Demonstrate running in place; they need to know how to do actions without smacking a neighbor!

As you lead the motions, move at a frantic pace, perhaps with a rehearsed volunteer assisting you. You'll begin with easy movements, increase activity, then cool down with easy actions again. Think of this as Aerobic Bible Review!

You can use this method with any Bible story you choose. Just tell the story and lead kids in accompanying motions. The following example of the story of Paul will give you a good idea of how to play the game.

Paul started as a student, reading scrolls *(make circular, unrolling motions with your hands)* and writing lots of pages. *(Pretend to scribble.)* Eventually he became a lawyer *(stand still, rubbing your chin thoughtfully)* who started looking for Christians to throw in jail. *(Peer around with your hand over your eyes.)*

He was on his way to Damascus *(walk quickly in place)* when he fell down blinded. *(Fall down and cover eyes.)* Then he became a Christian.

Later, Paul was beaten up *(pretend to be hit)*, shipwrecked *(pretend to be swimming)*, and robbed. *(Turn pockets inside out while jogging in place.)* Sometimes he was hungry *(rub stomach while jogging in place)*, and sometimes he was cold. *(Shiver and hug yourself.)* Once he even escaped over the wall of a city in a basket! *(Lower rope.)*

But he also had many chances to preach the Gospel. *(Stand and gesture with arms.)* He made many friends *(pretend to shake hands)* and helped many people believe in Jesus! *(Clap hands.)* Finally, he died and went home to be with the Lord. *(Look up and raise hands.)*

Add extra meaning to this game by asking children to consider the following questions as they cool down after the game:

● If someone were making a game about how we've suffered for Jesus, what actions could they use?

● If the game were about all the great things Jesus does for us, what actions could we use?

Bethlehem Balloons ———

Best For: Kindergarten through third grade
Energy Level: Medium
Supplies: An equal number of balloons in four colors, one balloon per child

The Fun:

Get ready for a flurry of balloons, and lots of laughter!

Ask children to inflate and tie off their balloons. Older children can help younger children who may have trouble completing this task.

Ask children to hold their balloons and sit on the floor. Situate children so they're equally spaced around your playing area. A room, or a specific area in a room, that's at least ten-by-ten feet works best for this game.

Announce that it's time to take a "census" of the balloons. Explain that a census is an official counting of a population. Tell kids it's time to count their balloon population!

Say that all balloons must be counted, and to be counted they must return to their "hometowns." The hometowns are the corners of your playing area. Designate which corners are the homes of which color balloons by assigning one color to each corner.

Tell kids that there's one catch with the balloon census: the balloons must be batted to the correct corners, and the children may not stand up or move from their spots.

Tell kids when to begin, then stand back and watch the fun! When all the balloons have been batted to the corners, close the game by asking each child to again take a balloon. Then let kids break their balloons by sitting (*not* stamping!) on them.

Add extra meaning to this game by referring to the story of the Roman census from Luke 2:1-5. Ask children:

● What was it like to move your balloon to a certain corner? How difficult or easy was this?

● How is that like how Joseph and Mary might have felt when they had to go to Bethlehem to be counted in a census? What do you think their trip was like?

feathered friends ━━━━

Best For: All ages
Energy Level: Low
Supplies: Construction paper, scrap paper, scissors, and masking
or transparent tape

The fun:

In this game, the kids will have a chance to cover their friends with feathers. Tie the game to a study on creation, or play it just for fun's sake!

Have kids form groups of four to six. Give each group a supply of scissors, construction paper, and scrap paper. Have each group choose one child to be a Feathered Friend. Each group will dress up its Feathered Friend for a gala "Feathered Friend Fashion Show." Have each group choose what kind of Feathered Friend it will represent. Groups might choose penguins, crows, flamingos, blue jays, or cardinals. Have groups cut out paper bird feathers, beaks, wings, and feet.

Have kids use masking or transparent tape to attach the feathers and other paper parts to the Feathered Friends. Show kids how to layer the feathers like scales for a fun effect. (Make sure kids don't use tape on delicate fabric that might be damaged by the adhesive.)

If you have plenty of time and paper, all of the kids in each group can dress up as a flock of feathered friends.

When the groups are finished decorating their Feathered Friends, have kids sit on either side of a pretend fashion runway in your classroom. Have each group choose an Announcer who will introduce the group's Feathered Friend. For example, an Announcer might say, "And here's Peter Penguin, dressed in an exquisite silk tuxedo, perfect for that special formal affair." Encourage kids to have fun with their commentaries.

Encourage the spectators to cheer each Feathered Friend on, while making the kind of birdcall that specific bird might make.

Penny Toss

Best For: First through fifth grade
Energy Level: Low
Supplies: Pennies, a cup or saucer, and three three-foot lengths of string

The Fun:

This is a game of skill...but it's a skill you'll be hard pressed to use!

Place a cup or saucer on the floor. Then lay the three lengths of string in three successive rows near the cup. One string should be three feet from the cup, one should be four feet from the cup, and the other five feet from the cup.

Give each child an equal number of pennies. Have children stand behind the closest line and let them try to toss pennies into the cup.

Don't give pennies to young children who are apt to put the pennies in their mouths, which presents a choking hazard.

Then have children stand behind the second line as they get better at scoring points. Use the third line if you have sharpshooters in your group!

For extra fun, have kids each say something they're thankful to God for as they toss each penny.

Answer Mat ———

Best For: Third through sixth grade
Energy Level: Low
Supplies: A sheet of newspaper

The Fun:

This game gives a new meaning to the phrase, "Fast on your feet!"

Spread the newspaper in the center of the floor. Ask children to gather around the paper. Explain that you're going to ask kids a few questions. Say that these questions actually have many answers. In fact, there are no "right" answers to these questions, and you want to hear lots of interesting answers.

Explain that when a child thinks of an answer to a question, the child will jump onto the newspaper Answer Mat and call out an answer. Then the child should quickly jump off the newspaper to give someone else a chance to answer. Let as many kids as want to jump on the Answer Mat for each question. Encourage children to participate, and stress that all answers are acceptable.

Possible questions might include:

● What's the one question you never want to hear from a teacher?

● What's the scariest thing you can think of?

● Who's the greatest cartoon hero?

● What's one thing no little brother or sister could possibly break?

● Which words rhyme with the word "sing"?

● Which words rhyme with the word "sky"?

● Which words are spelled the same forward and backward? (Pop, dad, bob, and mom are a few.)

● Which words rhyme with the word "orange"? (Close with this question!)

Two in the Ring ———

Best For: All ages
Energy Level: Medium
Supplies: Inflatable swim rings

The Fun:

This game is fun in itself, but would also be a great way to introduce a lesson on the Church as the body of Christ.

Form groups of about six. Have each group form a circle, and give each group an inflatable swim ring. Have someone in each group inflate the ring if you haven't already done so.

Call out "right arm," and have the person in each group who's holding the ring put his or her right arm through the ring. Then call out another appendage from the following list: left arm, right arm, left leg, right leg, head, left elbow, right elbow.

When you call out the body part, the person to the right of the person currently having the ring must put that body part through the ring also. The first person may need to bend or cooperate in some way for this to happen, but must not let the ring slide off of his or her right arm.

Once the first two people have the correct parts through the ring, call out another body part. At this point, the first person should remove his or her right arm from the ring, and the second person should turn to the third, who then puts the appropriate part through the ring. Continue until all kids have had at least two chances to pass the ring.

Make the game interesting by combining difficult body parts in the ring, such as right elbow and right leg, or head and left leg.

End the game by calling, "All left arms in the ring!" Then have kids give themselves a round of applause without removing their arms from the rings.

Matching Pairs ———

Best For: All ages
Energy Level: Medium
Supplies: Sheets of paper, marker, and tape

The Fun:

This game can help kids learn each other's names and names of Bible pairs at the same time.

Before the game, write on sheets of paper in large letters the names of several Bible pairs, one name per sheet. You might use pairs from the following list:

- Adam and Eve
- Cain and Abel
- Noah and the Ark
- Abraham and Sarah
- Isaac and Rebekah
- Jacob and Esau
- Samson and Delilah
- David and Goliath
- Mary and Joseph
- Mary and Martha
- Paul and Silas

This game is played similar to Concentration, but with several variations. Select eight kids to be the Matchers and have the rest of the kids be the Guessers.

¤ Game Guide

If you have fewer than ten children, reduce the number of pairs to match each round. If you have more than sixteen children, you might want to have more pairs to match for each round.

Have the Matchers line up with their backs toward a wall, about three feet away from the wall. Without letting anyone see the names, tape one name sheet to each Matcher's back, making sure the names complete four Bible pairs, but mixing them up in the line of kids. When you finish taping sheets to the Matchers' backs, have them step back against the wall, being careful not to let anyone see the names on their backs.

Have the Guessers take turns calling out two Matchers' names to try to match the Bible pairs. When a Matcher's name is called, he or she must turn around to reveal the name on his or her back. If the Bible names don't make a pair, the two Matchers turn back around. Once a pair has been matched, the kids bearing the names of the matched pair may join the Guessers.

After all four pairs have been matched, select eight more kids to be Matchers, and have the kids play the game again. Continue until everyone gets a chance to play both a Matcher and a Guesser.

¤Game Guide

If kids don't know each other's names well, have each child wear a name tag.

Jumpin' Jeopardy

Best For: Third through sixth grade
Energy Level: Medium
Supplies: Note cards and pencils

The Fun:

This is a great getting-to-know-you-better game.

Give each child two or three note cards. Have kids write on each note card something they enjoy doing or something they've done that few, if any, kids in the class know about. For example, someone might write, "Vacationed at the Grand Canyon when I was five," or "Like to fish for trout."

Gather all the cards and mix them thoroughly. Then read the statements on the cards one at a time. After each statement, have any kids jump up if they think they know who wrote the statement. Let the first child to jump up answer, but the answer must be in the form of a question, such as, "Who is Jamie?"

If the question identifies the correct person, the child who wrote the card must stand up as the class cheers. If the question is incorrect, the asker must sit down. Then the next child to jump up must try to guess the correct child in the same way.

After two incorrect questions, reveal the person who wrote the card by saying, for example, "Will the real Grand Canyon visitor please stand up?" At that point the child who wrote the card should stand, be cheered for, and then sit down.

Proceed with the game until you've read all the cards.

If you have fewer than six kids, you might want to give each child more note cards. If you have more than twenty kids, you might want to form groups of ten for this game.

A Penny for Your Thoughts ━━━━

Best For: All ages
Energy Level: Low
Supplies: Pennies

The Fun:

Want to find out what your kids are thinking? Just ask them! This game provides an easy way.

Explain to your children there was once a common saying, "A penny for your thoughts." Offer them the same deal. Ask kids questions such as the ones below, and give them a penny when they answer.

- What's your favorite food?
- Where would you most like to go on vacation?
- Would you rather have hamburgers or salad for lunch? Why?
- What famous person would you most like to meet?
- What do you think you do best?
- What's your favorite TV show? Why?
- How old do you want to be when you get married—if you want to get married? Why?
- If you could have any pet, what would it be?

Either let kids keep the pennies, or have kids return the pennies to a designated container in your classroom. That way, you'll always have a ready discussion-starter handy!

Word Spell ━━━━

Best For: Third through sixth grade
Energy Level: Low
Supplies: None

The Fun:

This is a great game to illustrate the benefits of working together.

Form groups of about six. Have each child think of a word that has the same number of letters as there are people in their groups. Caution kids not to let kids in other groups hear what their words are.

Have one child from the first group spell out his or her word for the other groups, using arm, leg, head, and body positions to create the letters one at a time. When the first word has been guessed, have someone from another group do the same thing. Repeat until two or three kids from each group have spelled out words. If you have time, let each child spell out a word.

Then tell kids they're going to work together to spell out the words. Have each group huddle and choose one word from the kids who haven't yet spelled a word (or a new word if everyone has had a turn to spell).

Then have the person whose word was chosen assign a letter to each group member. Have kids line up so the letters form the correct spelling of the word. Then have kids form their letters all at once.

Each group will have a turn to spell its word, while other groups try to guess the word.

¤ Game Guide

You may want to quietly go over the spelling of the words with children to avoid the embarrassment of misspelled words. Keep scrap paper handy to write the correct spelling of words for groups to refer to. You could also suggest that kids come up with words related to what you're studying.

An Introduction to Large Indoor-Space Games

Here they are! A new collection of noncompetitive, energetic, easy-to-lead games for your gymnasium. Let your kids romp and stomp through these fun and easy games, and they'll be more receptive to your teaching, and more willing to come back for more.

Don't have a gymnasium? Never fear—just clear the furniture from the center of any large room, and you'll be ready to roll with lots of these active games.

Make your children's ministry the best it can be by offering kids an element they may not expect at church—some good, old-fashioned, high-energy game playing!

Assembly Line Sundaes

Best For: Third through sixth grade
Energy Level: Low
Supplies: A long table; bowls; spoons; ice-cream scoops; and
supplies to make ice-cream sundaes, such as various
flavors of ice cream, syrups, nuts, chocolate chips,
whipped cream, and fruit

The Fun:

This game is a fun way to give your kids a nice, cool treat.

Set your ice-cream sundae supplies on a long table, spacing
the supplies so several kids can stand near each supply. Be sure
the ice cream is at one end of the table, or the starting place, and
the spoons are at the other end.

Depending on the size of your class, assign children sundae
supplies individually, in pairs, or in teams. Ideally, you'll have
enough children to have kids work in pairs. Have each pair stand
by the supply it has been assigned.

¤ Game Guide — If you have a variety of ages in your group,
try forming pairs or groups with mixed ages,
encouraging older children to work with and
help younger children.

Hand a bowl to the pair at the starting place, and have that
pair put several scoops of ice cream into the bowl. Then instruct
the kids to pass the bowl down the line, as other pairs fill it with
toppings and treats. At the end of the line, have the pair place a
spoon in the bowl. Continue to send bowls down the line as children build their ice-cream sundaes.

When the children have created a sundae for each person in
the group, encourage kids to sit down together and enjoy their
treats. As children are eating, congratulate them on how well
they worked together. You may want to discuss the idea that they
all needed each other to complete their tasty tasks.

Stress how each person had something to contribute to the
final product, just as each child has something to contribute to the

group. This game also serves as a great way to wind up a study or lesson about working together as parts of the body of Christ.

This game works well outside as a refresher on a hot summer day. But you can also make your sundaes inside. A large room, such as a fellowship hall, would be ideal. Just be sure you have plenty of paper towels on hand for quick cleanup!

Charades Relay

Best For: Third through sixth grade
Energy Level: High
Supplies: None

The Fun:

This high-energy game will encourage kids' creativity, and tire them out a little, too!

Have children form groups of three. Have half of the trios go to one side of the room, and half go to the other side of the room.

Choose a trio to begin the game. Have kids in that trio think of an object they would like to act out, such as a car or a sofa. When they've thought of their object, instruct the trio to work together to form a representation of it.

For example, if the trio decides to form a car, two children may crouch down to form "wheels" while the other child stands between the two "wheels" with his or her arms on the other two children, to form the body of the car. Be sure trios don't tell other groups what they've decided to represent.

For a group of younger children, you may want to make this game easier by instructing trios to portray animals instead of objects.

The trio must form this object, and at the same time, make its way across the floor to the opposite side of the room. As the trio is moving across the room, encourage the rest of the children to guess what the trio is trying to portray. If no one has guessed by the time the trio reaches the other side of the room, let the trio announce what it was portraying to the class.

Then have a trio from the other side of the room form an object and begin making its way across the room. Continue until all trios have taken a turn or until everyone is worn out!

Design-Your-Own Obstacle Course ———

Best For: Third through sixth grade
Energy Level: High
Supplies: Newsprint; markers; and various obstacles such as chairs, tables, boxes, ropes, athletic equipment, hymn books, and blankets

The Fun:

This game calls for plenty of room, creative ideas, and lots of energy!

Have children form groups of three to five. Explain to the children that groups will each take a turn creating an obstacle course for the rest of the class to follow. Then show children the obstacle supplies available for groups to use to create their courses. Each group can plan to use all of the supplies available.

¤ Game Guide	If you have a small group, a shortage of time, or a small room, you may want to have kids design an obstacle course as one large group, rather than breaking into small groups.

Give each group a piece of newsprint and a marker. Instruct each group to design its own obstacle course and draw a diagram of the course on the piece of newsprint. Encourage each group to include at least four stations in its obstacle course and to use only the supplies you've provided or designated. You might want to let groups name their obstacles.

While kids are planning their obstacle courses, circulate among the groups, and discuss their plans with them. Be sure each obstacle course will be safe and practical.

When kids have designed their courses, have them take turns setting up their courses and leading the other groups in completing their courses. As the children are completing the courses, encourage them to cheer on one another. End each obstacle course with a loud group cheer.

¤ Game Guide

If you want to use this game as an object lesson, instruct groups to design their obstacle-course stations so they represent actual obstacles they encounter in real life, such as fear, anger, and temptation. As they go through the obstacle courses, lead kids in discussing how Jesus can help them overcome obstacles they face. You may want to encourage kids to brainstorm about biblical verses that remind them how Jesus can help them.

Back-sket Ball ━━━

Best For: All ages
Energy Level: High
Supplies: Four different colors of balloons, four laundry baskets, and an electric fan (optional)

The Fun:

Before the game, have kids help you inflate and tie off about ten to fifteen balloons of each color. Then let children scatter the balloons around the playing area. Place each laundry basket in a different corner of the room. Then have kids form four groups, and have each group stand by a laundry basket.

Assign each group a color that corresponds to a balloon color. When you say "go," each group will try to collect its color balloons and deposit them in its laundry basket. Tell kids that it would be pretty easy if they could just run around the room and collect them, but instead, kids will have to crab-walk!

Kids will have to balance the balloons on their tummies, or hold the balloons between their knees as they transport the balloons to the baskets. Caution kids not to hold balloons with their mouths.

Alert kids that you'll be timing them to see how long it takes for all the groups to collect their balloons. Then in the next round, kids can try to beat that time!

Start your timer and let kids begin. For an added challenge, you may want to place several electric fans around the room to blow the balloons about! Play two or three times, encouraging kids to beat the clock!

Balloon Blitz ———

Best For: All ages
Energy Level: Medium
Supplies: Balloons and trash bags

The Fun:

This game is a great way to build teamwork and cooperation. It can also be used to show kids how life can get too busy and out of control.

Before the game, blow up and tie off one balloon for each child. Put all the inflated balloons in a trash bag. If you have a large class, use more trash bags. Have your kids join you in forming a tight circle. Put the bag of balloons in the center of the circle.

Take out one balloon, and tap it to the child next to you. Explain to kids that the goal of the game is to keep the balloons moving and up in the air at all times. Say that if a balloon hits the ground, the nearest person should pick it up and keep it moving.

Have kids continue tapping the balloon to each other while you add more balloons. See how many balloons the kids can keep going before the game reaches total chaos. Once the game is out of control, collect the balloons and begin again. Count how many balloons kids are able to calmly keep in the air.

As a simple object lesson, encourage kids to name the balloons for the many activities they have to juggle in real life. Then discuss how they can look to God for help in every situation.

Chain Gang ——

Best For: All ages
Energy Level: Medium
Supplies: None

The Fun:

This game is a great icebreaker, or it can be used to help kids bond as a group.

Tell kids that they're going to create a gigantic chain. Instruct kids to use items they brought to the meeting or items in the classroom area to create the chain.

For example, kids could unlace their shoes and tie the laces to the chain, tie their jackets to the chain, use key chains, or even use their socks! From the classroom, kids might use rubber bands, paper clips, tape, yarn, hangers, or any other safe supply you have available.

Encourage everyone to participate by adding whatever items they can find. Challenge kids to make the chain as long and as creative as possible.

After the chain is finished, applaud kids' ingenuity and cooperation. Take note of creative additions of unusual items. You might want to measure the chain, and even take a picture of it as a testament to your kids' creativity. (Make sure to give kids a chance at some "creative cleanup" by asking them to take the chain apart and put the items away when you're finished!)

Use the chain as a way to encourage kids by reminding them that just as each person contributed to the chain, each person has a gift from God to contribute to the good of God's family.

Tightrope

Best For: All ages
Energy Level: High
Supplies: Blindfolds

The Fun:

This game can be used to help kids see how we need each other's help to make it in life.

Have kids form pairs. Mark off boundaries that are large enough for all your kids to stand in with their hands outstretched so no one is touching. Explain to your kids that half of them are going to wear blindfolds to play the game. Tell children that the people wearing blindfolds are to walk by placing one foot in front of the other, as if on a tightrope.

Explain that the children without the blindfolds are responsible for directing their partners. The kids without blindfolds can direct their partners by using verbal commands or by gently pushing on one of their shoulders with one finger.

Point out the boundaries kids shouldn't cross. Give one blindfold to each pair of kids and have pairs decide who will wear the blindfold first. Direct kids to put on the blindfolds.

Ask one of the pairs to act as the Tightrope Taggers. The Tightrope Taggers will move around the area in the same manner as all the others pairs, but the blindfolded Tagger will try to tag any of the other blindfolded children. Once a person is tagged, that pair will act as the Tightrope Taggers. Let kids play long enough for most of the pairs to have a chance to be Taggers; then have kids switch roles with their partners.

 **Game Guide** To challenge older kids, don't allow children to touch their partners to give them direction.

Timing Is Everything

Best For: All ages
Energy Level: Medium
Supplies: A watch with a second hand or a stopwatch, scraps of paper, and pencils

The Fun:

Play this guessing game with your kids to exercise the important skill of estimation.

Tell kids you're going to explain a new game to them. Ask them to guess how long it will take you to explain it. Pass out scraps of paper and pencils. Have the children write down how many seconds they think it will take you to explain the game.

Start your timer when you begin explaining the game. When you finish explaining, stop your timer, and see how close their guesses came to the actual time elapsed.

Then explain that you're going to have kids do various activities. Before each activity, have kids write down an estimation of how long it will take them to do the various activities. Feel free to choose from the following list of activities, or make up your own.

Possible activities include:
- five push-ups,
- stacking all the chairs in the room,
- filling a pot with water,
- skipping twice around the room,
- taking off and putting back on their shoes and socks, or
- looking up a Bible verse.

Then time each activity. The kids will enjoy finding out how close their estimates were to the actual time.

Balloon Shepherding ———

Best For: Third through sixth grade
Energy Level: High
Supplies: One balloon per child, one section of newspaper per child, masking tape, two chairs, a stopwatch or watch with a second hand, and an electric fan

The Fun:

Do you think herding sheep is easy? This game will give your kids a feel of what it might be like to be shepherds as they try to herd a flock of balloons through a gate!

Give each child a newspaper section. Show children how to roll their newspaper sections into tightly rolled tubes. Have kids wrap strips of masking tape around the tubes to make stiff paper "staffs." Make sure kids understand the following guidelines:

● Safety is important! Tell kids there is to be no hitting, touching, or waving of the staffs!

● When you ask for the staffs to be returned to you, ask kids to return them to you quickly and safely.

To play the game, set up two chairs at one end of the room, three feet apart. The chairs will represent a gate through which your children will herd their balloon sheep. Place a masking-tape starting line on the floor at the opposite end of the room.

Give each child a balloon, and ask children to inflate and tie off their balloons. Older children can help younger children who may have trouble completing this task.

When each child has an inflated balloon, ask children to place their balloons on the floor, between their feet.

Explain that there are lots of shepherds mentioned in the Bible: David, Moses, and the shepherds who visited baby Jesus, to name a few. Remind kids that Jesus describes himself as the Good Shepherd.

Tell kids they're going to have a chance to be shepherds! Explain that when you say "go," kids will use their staffs to gently herd their balloon sheep across the room and through the gate. Tell kids they'll have sixty seconds to get all the sheep through the gate. Encourage kids to help each other and work together to guide their sheep where they need to be.

Begin the game, then stand back: A balloon avalanche is headed your way!

After sixty seconds, have kids return to the starting line for a second round. Set out the electric fan and place it on the lowest setting behind your two chairs. Turn the fan so the air will blow balloons back toward the starting line. Then have kids play the game again. After the game, compare the two methods of play.

Add extra meaning to this game with the following questions. Ask:

● Was shepherding your balloon easier or harder than you expected? Why?

● What does a real shepherd do for his sheep?

● Jesus said he's our Good Shepherd. Do we always go where he wants us to go? Explain.

● What can happen to sheep when they don't want to go where their shepherd leads? What happens when we don't follow Jesus?

Telephone Tag ━━━

Best For: Second through sixth grade
Energy Level: High
Supplies: A telephone book

The Fun:

If your kids know their phone numbers, they're ready for this number-memory game!

Place a telephone book in the middle of your playing area. Ask for a volunteer to begin the game. The volunteer will be the Caller. Have the Caller stand on the phone book. Have the other children scatter around the playing area.

Then have the Caller call out a number between one and nine. If the number is among the last four digits of a child's home phone number, that child must touch the phone book (with a foot) before being tagged by the Caller. Only those children who have the number appearing in their phone numbers will move.

The first child tagged will become the new Caller. If no one is tagged, the Caller should use a different number in the next round of play.

For subsequent rounds, vary the number of digits in the home phone number the children need to respond to. For example, only children who have the called number as one of the first three digits in their phone numbers might respond.

Static Statues ━━━

Best For: All ages
Energy Level: High
Supplies: Inflated balloons and paper grocery sacks

The Fun:

Form groups of no more than four and have groups line up on one side of the room. Give each group a paper grocery sack filled with inflated balloons.

Say that when God created the world, God made lots of fun creatures. Have kids tell the people in their groups their favorite creatures. Allow thirty seconds for kids to share, and then continue.

Explain that in this relay, each group will use its balloons to create a creature on the opposite wall. Tell kids you'll give them a few seconds to decide which animal they'll build. When you say "go," kids will take turns racing to the wall with a balloon.

When a child reaches the wall, he or she will rub the balloon on his or her head to build up lots of static electricity. Then the child will stick the balloon to the wall. The child will hurry back to the line, give the next person a high-five, and that child will add a balloon to the first balloon. As each child adds a balloon, the animal will take shape.

Give groups a few seconds to choose an animal. Then begin the game. When all groups have finished creating, allow children to guess what animal each group made.

Mooove Over Here! ━━

Best For: All ages
Energy Level: Medium
Supplies: None

The Fun:

Have children stand in a circle. Whisper the name of one of these animals, in order, to each of your children as you go around the group: Cow, Dog, Chicken, Pig, or Sheep.

Tell kids that when you say "go," kids will each make the sounds of the animals they've been assigned. Then kids will form groups with other animals like themselves. For examples, all the Cows will form a group, all the Dogs will form another group, and so on.

The trick to this game is that kids must not talk and must keep their eyes closed as they're searching for other animals of their kind. Advise kids that when they find another like animal, it's smart to grab that person's hand so they aren't separated.

Give children sixty seconds to find their animal partners. Clap your hands to call the game to a close. Help children who haven't yet found their groups connect with their animal partners.

Then add extra meaning to this game by asking groups of children to discuss these questions:

● How did you find each other?

● How do you pick your friends when you meet so many people every day?

● How can the Bible help you make choices?

Balloon Launch

Best For: Third through sixth grade
Energy Level: Medium
Supplies: Five balloons, a dark plastic trash bag, and a damp all-cotton mop head

The Fun:

What goes up must come down...and that includes balloons! See how well your kids can direct the landing of their balloons in this fun "flight of fancy."

Before class, blow up and tie off five balloons. Also, dampen an all-cotton (no metal parts) mop head, and place it in a dark plastic trash bag. Place the bag someplace inconspicuous near your playing area. The bag should be easily accessible by you during the game.

Have children sit in a circle. Explain that the goal of the game is to bat a balloon up in the air and to keep it from hitting the floor. Demonstrate how to gently bat a balloon so it floats over the circle—making it easy for other children to bat.

Launch one balloon, get a rhythm going, and then compliment your kids on their great effort. Then toss another balloon into the center of the circle. Add up to five balloons; then surprise kids by tossing the damp mop head into the circle to be batted about. (This should elicit lots of surprised laughs.)

Add extra meaning to this game by asking children:

● How did you feel when I kept adding balloons?

● How was this game like when you're busy with lots of things to do?

● What can you do to help the situation when you're stressed in real life?

Food Chain

Best For: Third through sixth grade
Energy Level: Low
Supplies: String or masking tape

The Fun:

This fun game can easily double as an icebreaker and crowd-breaker.

Before the game, use masking tape or string to make a line on the floor of your playing area. Make sure the line is long enough so everyone in your class can stand on the line at the same time.

Ask children to each choose a creature or plant of some sort. Kids may choose insects, mammals, plants, or any other living creation they want. Then ask your kids to line up on the line in order of the food chain—who eats what?

Give children sixty seconds to get in line; then let kids each tell what animal or plant they chose. See how well they estimated the order of the food chain; then have kids realign themselves accordingly. Discuss with your kids how God's creation works together.

Hip Hop!

Best For: Kindergarten through second grade
Energy Level: High
Supplies: String or masking tape

The Fun:

This energetic game will keep your class hopping!

Before the game, use masking tape or string to make a starting line and a finish line at opposite ends of your playing area. Have children line up at the starting line. Explain to kids that they're going to race to the finish line, but there's a catch: they have to hop like frogs!

Let them hop once straight through to the finish line so they understand the idea. Then explain that frogs are sometimes forgetful.

Tell children they're going to hop the race again, but this time they may have to hop back to the starting line to get things they forgot. Explain that they may have to turn around and hop back a time or two. Tell kids to listen carefully to your story as they hop so they know what to do.

Tell a story similar to the following tale. Have kids get in hopping position before you begin.

Freddy Froglegs decides to visit his cousin, Thelma Toad. So off he hops. *(Have kids begin hopping forward.)* But then he remembers he forgot his toothbrush! *(Have kids hop back.)* So Freddy takes off again with his toothbrush. *(Hop forward.)* But he forgot his pajamas! *(Hop back.)*

Now Freddy is on his way again. *(Hop forward.)* Everything is fine. *(Hop forward.)* What a pretty day! *(Hop forward.)* Wait! *(Stop.)* Freddy forgot his special "frog soap"! *(Hop back.)* No! Wait! *(Stop.)* Thelma will have some! Freddy keeps going to Thelma's house. *(Hop forward.)*

Hold it! *(Stop.)* He left the present he bought for Thelma on his table! *(Hop back.)* No, wait! *(Stop.)* He can buy her a new present at Toads 'R' Us in Thelma's town. *(Hop forward.)*

Hold it! *(Stop.)* He dropped his toothbrush. Got to go back to pick it up. *(Hop back.)* Got it. Now Freddy can finally get to Thelma's. *(Hop forward.)* Yea! There's her house. He's finally there! *(Stop.)*

The good news is your kids will love playing this game, and burn up lots of energy in the process. (The bad news is they may want to play it again and again!)

Keep It Up! ———

Best For: All ages
Energy Level: High
Supplies: A large balloon or volleyball, and tape or string

The Fun:

This game will give you a great way to foster cooperation and group spirit.

Because of skill level, you'll probably want to use a balloon for this game unless most of your kids are in the fourth grade or older. Divide your playing area into as many sections as you have kids, using already existing lines, tape, or string. Have each person stand inside one of the sections.

If you have fewer than ten kids, you may want to limit the size of your court by only using half of the gymnasium.

The object of this game is to keep the balloon or ball in the air for as long as possible before it touches the floor. Children will bat the balloon or ball to each other, volleyball-style. No one may step out of his or her section, and no one may hit the balloon or ball back to the person they received it from.

Remind kids that the goal is to keep the ball or balloon in the air for as many hits as possible, not to make the ball or balloon hit the floor in someone else's section.

Have kids keep count of how many times the ball or balloon is batted, shouting out the number each time it's hit. Each time the ball or balloon does hit the floor, have kids switch places so kids around the outside of the playing area move to the inside, where there is more action. Be sure no one receives criticism or put-downs for letting the ball or balloon drop in his or her section.

If you're using a balloon, you may want to allow kids to hit it more than once in their own sections to be able to get it to another person. However, count only one hit for any one person while the balloon is in his or her section.

Oddball Bowling

Best For: All ages
Energy Level: High
Supplies: A volleyball, a small bag of sunflower seeds or candies, nine empty two-liter plastic bottles, and duct tape or packing tape

The Fun:

Use this game as a fun way to introduce the values of patience and determination.

Before the game, use duct tape or packing tape to secure a small bag of sunflower seeds or small candies to the side of a volleyball. Form two groups and have them line up at opposite ends of the playing area.

Set up the nine two-liter bottles like bowling pins in the middle of your playing area, only set them up in a square.

¤ Game Guide — If you have more than nineteen kids, use one ball and set of pins for every ten children.

Tell kids that as soon as they have worked together to knock down ninety-nine pins, you'll have a treat for everyone. Give the volleyball to the first person in line at one end of the gym, and have that person roll the ball and knock down as many pins as possible.

Have the first person in line at the other end of the gym retrieve the ball and roll it back at the pins. Keep alternating teams until all the pins are down. Then reset them and have kids go at it again. Encourage kids to cheer for each other since every pin knocked down gets them one step closer to their treat.

Keep track of the total number of pins knocked down. When your total reaches ninety-nine, stop the game, and serve the seeds or candy that was taped to the volleyball. Depending on the size of your group, you may want to have more candy available to serve.

¤ Game Guide — The purpose of the bag taped to the side of the ball is to make it off-balanced so it will roll erratically. You could also use a small bag of unpopped popcorn or nuts. It just needs to add significant weight to one side of the ball and to create a fun snack for the kids.

Switcheroo! ━━━━

Best For: Third through sixth grade
Energy Level: Low
Supplies: Masking tape

The Fun:

This game provides a great way to help kids build group identity while fostering a real spirit of cooperation.

Place two long strips of masking tape parallel to each other, about eight inches apart. The lines will need to be long enough to give each person a place to stand on them.

Have kids line up on the tape lines according to when their birthdays are. Kids with January birthdays will be on one end; kids with December birthdays will be on the other end. Kids should stand with one foot on each line. Make sure the kids are all facing in the same direction.

Tell kids that you want them to pull a "switcheroo" by reversing their positions. That is, you want the January and December birthdays to switch places, and everyone in between to arrange themselves in sequence again. That means some kids will be moving forward, and some will be moving backward. Kids will each need to move to the opposite end of the lines, but they need to stay facing in the same direction, and they can only step on the lines (not off the lines).

Kids will need to help each other move along the line in any way possible, helping each other balance and holding on to each other. They'll also need to communicate verbally with each other, both to alert each other as to their next actions and to make sure they're arranged properly by birthday.

When the "switcheroo" is complete, the line of kids will be a mirror image of the initial line.

To add more challenge, have the kids line up randomly on the tape lines. Then tell them to switch places and line themselves up according to birthdays, with kids with January birthdays at one end and kids with December birthdays at the other.

After the game, discuss with kids how the Bible tells us we're to help and encourage one another, just as they did in the game.

Horse Sense ———

Best For: All ages
Energy Level: High
Supplies: Sticks such as brooms, hockey sticks, or yardsticks; a small ball; two chairs or a table; and a stopwatch or watch with a second hand

The Fun:

This active game encourages everyone to get involved!

Set up a goal at one end of your playing area. You might set two chairs next to each other about three feet apart, or set a table at one end of the room. Explain to kids that the space between the chairs or under the table is the goal.

Have kids gather at the other end of the playing area. Give each player a stick such as a broom, a hockey stick, or a yardstick. It's OK to have a variety of sticks, as long as everyone has one. Have players hold sticks between their legs as if they were riding pretend horses. Caution kids to keep the sticks in place and not to wave them in the air where they could injure others.

Explain that the part of the sticks that are touching the floor are the "tails." Hold up the ball for all to see, and explain that you'll drop the ball on the floor. Each person must use his or her tail to move the ball closer to the goal. Explain that the ball cannot pass through the goal until each person has hit the ball at least once.

Toss the ball in front of the group of kids, call "go!" and begin timing. As soon as the ball has been hit by each player's tail and has passed through the goal, call time.

¤ Game Guide

If you're playing with a variety of sticks, trade sticks after each round. Obviously the brooms are easiest to hit the balls with, while the yard-sticks are the hardest. Be sure to trade around so everyone is challenged at various levels!

Play several more rounds, seeing if kids can beat their previous times. As they play, kids may become more organized and develop a strategy for getting the ball passed to each player and through the goal.

If the game seems too easy, add a second (or even third) ball of a different kind. Each child must hit both balls with his or her tail.

¤ Game Guide

Use a larger ball, such as a beach ball, when playing with younger children. Older children can handle the challenge of smaller balls such as tennis balls. For an even bigger challenge, use a table tennis ball!

Balloon Rally ————

Best For: Third through sixth grade
Energy Level: High
Supplies: Balloons and permanent markers

The Fun:

This is a fun game in itself, but could take a deeper direction if you so choose. Use this game when you're teaching what life is like without God's direction.

Clear the middle of your classroom, and have kids stand on one side of the room. Give every student a balloon. Make certain the balloons are easy for children to blow up. Have kids use permanent markers to write their names on their balloons before you begin the game.

Explain that the entire group needs to get to the other side of the classroom by blowing up their balloons, letting them go, going to where they landed, and launching them again. Give the entire group one minute to reach the other side of the classroom. Extend the time period if only one student hasn't made it to the other side of the classroom.

Talk about how the balloons didn't go where kids thought they would, and how much harder it was to get to the other side of the room using the balloons, rather than just walking in a straight line. Discuss how, unless we follow God's direction, our lives are more difficult and don't go in the direction we want them to.

Hula Hi-Jinks ————

Best For: Third through sixth grade
Energy Level: High
Supplies: A Hula Hoop and small beanbags or balls (such as tennis balls)

The Fun:

This wacky game gets kids really running!

Give each child one ball or beanbag. Have kids gather at one side of the room. Explain that you'll roll the Hula Hoop across the room. (Just give it a good throw and watch it roll!)

The goal of the game is for kids to see how many times they can toss their balls through the hoop before the hoop falls over. After a ball is tossed, kids can run and retrieve their balls, and if they are able, throw it through the hoop again.

When the hoop falls, add up how many times each child got a ball through the hoop. Kids will have to help by keeping track of how many times they tossed a ball through. Play again, seeing if kids can top their previous numbers.

If the balls or beanbags you're using all look the same, allow kids to pick up any ball to use again. Older kids might even figure out strategies of working together, throwing the ball back and forth to each other through the hoop.

For a quieter game, have kids sit in a row, and roll the hoop past them. See if each child can throw his or her ball through the hoop as it passes. Play again and again, aiming for 100 percent of the balls going through the hoop before it falls.

Potato Promenade ━━━

Best For: Second through sixth grade
Energy Level: Medium
Supplies: A small potato and a watch with a second hand

The Fun:

This game provides personal challenges as well as opportunities to cheer for others!

Form two groups, and have these groups stand in lines at opposite ends of the gym. Take a potato and demonstrate the following procedure.

⍺ Game Guide If you have a large number of children, form several groups, giving each group its own potato.

Place your feet closely together. Set the potato on top of your feet. Carefully shuffle your feet so you move forward, keeping the potato balanced on the tops of your feet.

After everyone has seen your demonstration, give the first person in one of the lines the potato. The idea is for this person to shuffle along to the first person in the opposite line, pass off the potato, then have that person shuffle back to the next person in the first line. Keep track of the time it takes for everyone to

promenade with the potato; then have kids play again. Encourage groups to race against their previous times.

If children have trouble keeping the potato on top of their feet, allow them to place it on the floor between their feet and move by waddling with both feet always touching the potato.

The younger the children, the closer together you should move your opposing lines. If young children have to go across a huge gym floor they'll get frustrated, and those waiting in line will get bored. You might try starting with kids about ten feet apart, and make the lines closer or farther apart in following rounds depending on how kids do.

An Introduction to Outdoor Games

What's more fun than playing inside? Playing outside!

When your kids are bursting with energy, just pick up this book and head for the great outdoors.

You'll find Hula Hoops, beach balls, balloons, and more! And you'll also find lots of games that don't require any prep or props at all. These games will help your kids build friendships as they build confidence at the same time.

No more being chosen last in Dodge Ball. Your kids will learn to cooperate and have plenty of fun—without put-downs!

Wiggleworm ━━━━

Best For: All ages
Energy Level: High
Supplies: Jump-ropes and a foam ball

The Fun:

Before the game, use jump-ropes to mark off a large square or rectangular area in your playing area. Choose one child to be the Tagger, and have the Tagger stand outside the playing area.

Instruct the rest of the group to form a line inside the square, having each person hold the shoulders of the person in front of him or her. This is the Wiggleworm! Hand the foam ball to the Tagger, and explain that the Tagger will stand outside the jump-rope lines and use the ball to try to tag someone in the Wiggleworm.

Members of the Wiggleworm will have to work together to wiggle all around to avoid being tagged! If someone is tagged, he or she becomes the Tagger and the person who was the Tagger may join the Wiggleworm.

For added variety, you might make several Wiggleworms or have more than one person be a Tagger.

Barrel of Monkeys ━━━

Best For: All ages
Energy Level: High
Supplies: None

The Fun:

This game is great for building up friendships and breaking down cliques in your group.

Have kids form pairs, lock arms with their partners, and stand at a distance from other pairs. If you have an uneven number of children, join the game yourself! Choose one pair, and designate one person in that pair to be the Gorilla and his or her partner to be the Monkey. Everyone else is a Monkey. Have the Monkey and the Gorilla separate and move to opposite sides of the room.

Explain that the Gorilla's goal is to tag the Monkey. Once the Monkey has been tagged, the Monkey becomes the new Gorilla and will chase the person who tagged him or her. The Monkey will be safe from being tagged by the Gorilla when he or she connects arms with any of the pairs of Monkeys that are scattered around the area.

Explain that once a Monkey who is being chased connects arms with a pair of Monkeys, the Monkey on the outside of the trio is no longer safe from the Gorilla. That Monkey must run to another pair and lock arms with one of the Monkeys. The Monkey on the outside of that trio must then run from the Gorilla.

¤ Game Guide For extra fun, have more than one person act as the Gorilla.

Bombs Away! ━━━━

Best For: Third through sixth grade
Energy Level: High
Supplies: Balloons, water, buckets, and old twin bedsheets or towels

The Fun:

This game is a great way to cool off on a hot summer day.

Before this activity, fill up balloons with water, and tie them off. Use buckets to transport the balloons outside.

Have kids form equal groups of four to eight, depending on the size of your class. Have each group surround an old bedsheet. Have groups number off and instruct each group to stay within five feet of the other groups. If you have groups of four or less, you might want to use old towels, rather than bedsheets.

Put a water balloon in the middle of Group 1's sheet. Have group members of Group 1 launch the balloon to Group 2 by quickly pulling the sheet taut. Have Group 2 attempt to catch the balloon and then pass it on to the next group. When all of the balloons have been launched and have either broken or reached the last group's sheet, have kids launch them down the line in the other direction.

For extra fun, have the groups spread out farther from each other as kids get the hang of launching the balloons. You could also have kids launch the balloons faster and faster. Another fun variation is to have the last group begin launching balloons back down the line as soon as they receive them. That way you'll have balloons going in both directions at once!

Hoopla

Best For: All ages
Energy Level: Medium
Supplies: A Hula Hoop and individually wrapped candies

The fun:

Have kids form two lines, about five feet apart. Kids should sit facing each other so each child has a partner sitting directly across from him or her. Have the first pair of children in line stand, one at either end of the line. Demonstrate how to quickly roll the hoop between the two lines.

Then give each person sitting in line a handful of candy. Have the kids standing roll the Hula Hoop between the lines. As the hoop is rolling, the kids will try to toss their candies through the hoop to their partners.

Let kids take turns rolling the hoop to their partners. For an added challenge, have the "hoop rollers" roll two hoops in opposite directions. After the fun, let kids enjoy the candy.

¤Game Guide If the wrappers have come off any of the candies, make sure to give kids fresh treats.

Esau and Jacob

Best For: All ages
Energy Level: High
Supplies: Blindfold

The Fun:

Play this fun game to give kids an idea what Isaac might have felt like when he tried to give his blessing to Esau.

Clear your playing area of any obstructions that might trip a player. Designate the boundaries of your playing area. (Keep your playing area fairly small to ensure your blindfolded player won't have too tough a time tagging someone else.) Show kids the "out of bounds" borders. You may need to assign kids to take turns monitoring these borders.

Emphasize that no running is allowed in this game. Choose one volunteer to be Isaac. All of the other kids will be Jacobs. Carefully blindfold Isaac.

Isaac will stand in the middle of the other players and shout "Esau!" The Jacobs should respond by saying, "Jacob." Remind the players they must say "Jacob" whenever Isaac says "Esau." The blindfolded Isaac will use the sound of the answering voices to try to tag a Jacob. The player he tags will become the next Isaac.

For a fun variation of this game, have all of the Jacobs hold hands and cooperate to keep away from Isaac. The player who is touched by Isaac will then leave the Jacob line and hold hands with Isaac. As the game continues, the Isaac line will get larger and larger as the Jacob line gets smaller.

Follow the Leveler

Best For: All ages
Energy Level: Medium
Supplies: None

The Fun:

This version of Follow the Leader is for the levelheaded player!

Choose a volunteer to be the Leveler. Have kids line up behind the Leveler. Have children try to position themselves so their heads are level with the children's heads in front of them. The object of the game is for children to stay in line and keep their heads level with the heads in front of them.

Ask the Leveler to walk around the room and change the position of his or her head, up and down, side to side, and so on. The Leveler can change the speed and method of travel, too. He or she can jog, hop, and even go under tables!

Wolves and Sheep

Best For: All ages
Energy Level: High
Supplies: Green construction paper

The Fun:

This game requires a high level of cooperation to keep the Wolves away from the Sheep!

Let kids tear a few sheets of green construction paper into medium-sized pieces. These paper pieces will be the leaves that the Sheep will try to "eat."

Depending on the size of your class, choose one to three children to be the Wolves. (If you have a small class, choose only one Wolf.) Then choose one to three children to be Sheep. The rest of the children will join hands and form a circle (the sheepfold).

Distribute the "leaves" outside the circle. The Wolves will stand outside the circle, and the Sheep will stand inside the circle.

The object of the game is for the Sheep to dart outside the fold to get the leaves without being caught by the Wolves. The

Wolves will roam around the sheepfold waiting for the Sheep to attempt to get the leaves.

The children forming the sheepfold should cooperate to keep the Wolves away from the Sheep. They can raise their hands to let the Sheep in and out, and lower their hands to stop the Wolves from catching the Sheep.

After the Sheep gather all of the leaves, or after the Wolves catch all of the Sheep, select new Wolves, and have the kids play again.

Remote Control ━━━━

Best For: Second through sixth grade
Energy Level: Medium
Supplies: None

The fun:

Do you ever wish you had a remote control that could just freeze your kids in place? Here's your chance…and you don't even need batteries!

Have kids form groups of five or six, and arrange groups all around you so you're in the center of the groups.

Explain that you're holding an invisible remote control, and each group is a television set. (For extra fun, bring a real remote control device from home, or hold a ruler or other object during the game.) The goal of each group is to create a scene that looks like the type of TV show you're punching up on your remote control.

Groups will have thirty seconds to get in place; then they'll freeze as you point your remote control at them and hit your "pause" button. Since only one group at a time will freeze, all the other groups will enjoy watching the action.

Use the following types of TV programs to get started, or think of your own shows.

- A football game
- The National Tug of War finals
- A church service
- A movie about the wild west
- A news story about a fireman rescuing a cat
- A cooking show
- A nature show about fish

- A cartoon about snowmen
- A sing-along children's show

¤ Game Guide

Add extra meaning to this game by suggesting that kids act out a church service. Then ask these questions:
- Why did you act out church the way you did?
- What would make church mean more to you?

Human Croquet ━━━━

Best For: First through fourth grade
Energy Level: High
Supplies: A soft inflated ball

The Fun:

This game works well to foster cooperation in a normally competitive setting.

Set up a human croquet course, having kids be the Wickets. If you have more than twenty-four kids, have two children stand facing each other and join hands to form each Wicket. If you have twelve to twenty-four kids, have one child form each Wicket by standing with feet apart, or by kneeling on hands and knees. If you have fewer than twelve children, set up a simplified course based on how many kids you have. You'll want at least two children to be players at all times. If you have a large group, you may have more than two players.

Once your course is set up, explain that no one is competing to beat anyone else in this game. The purpose is to help everyone win. So as the ball is kicked toward a Wicket, that Wicket should move to let the ball go through it if it's at all possible.

¤Game Guide

Caution kids to kick the ball gently so as not to hurt the kids playing the Wickets.

Have the players take turns, one kick per turn, until they get the ball all the way through the course. Then have players change places with Wickets. Keep playing at least until everyone has had a chance to be both a Wicket and a player.

¤Game Guide

If you end up with more than five players in your game, use one ball for every three players. Have each group of players start after the group ahead of it has kicked the ball through the second Wicket. This will move the play along faster and give more kids opportunities to be players.

March This Way

Best For: Kindergarten through second grade
Energy Level: High
Supplies: Two adult volunteers

The Fun:

Very young children love to play Follow the Leader if the game is fun...and you'll make this game a blast! Here's how.

Ask children to form a single file line. Position one adult leader at the end of the line, and another in the middle of the line. Tell children they'll follow the Leader who is holding up his or her hand.

Stand at the head of the line and hold up your hand. You'll be the first Leader, and the line will march behind you. Vary the pace from slow to almost double time. Keep holding up your hand.

Eventually, form a circle. Have the adult you placed at the end of the line march directly ahead of you. Tap that adult on the shoulder to signal that he or she will hold up a hand as you lower yours; then step out of the line. That adult will become the Leader and children will follow that person. Join them by tagging on to the end of the line.

After a few laps around the area, the adult in the middle of the line will hold up a hand to become the third Leader, and the second Leader will lower his or her hand. Help the kids scramble into a line after the third Leader. Great confusion and noise will commence, and that's part of the fun. Direct kids and aim them after the new Leader.

Move into a circle again and slow the pace to cool down. Then sit in a circle and lead your kids in giving themselves a big round of applause for following.

Scipmylo ━━━

Best For: All ages
Energy Level: High
Supplies: Water balloons and flour

The Fun:

Scipmylo...that's "Olympics" spelled backward—which pretty much describes this game! Announce to your kids that they've all been selected to compete in the Scipmylo. It's a backward Olympics!

Form groups of four, and let your kids try these silly events:

● **Say the alphabet...backward!**

● **Run a relay race...backward!** Using flour, create two lines on the field, twenty yards apart. Have half of the kids line up on one line, with their partners lining up across from them on the opposite line.

Tell children on the first line that they must speed-walk backward to their partners on the other line. Players from one line will speed-walk backward to the second line, and then their partners will speed-walk back to the first line, relay style.

¤ Game Guide

Explain that although they can't turn around while traveling, kids can look over their shoulders to see where they're going.

● **Walk the line...backward!** Place your children at the end of one of your relay lines. See if they can walk on the line, backward, without looking behind them.

● **Toss and catch water balloons...backward!** Ask older children to form pairs. Give the partner who is wearing the most blue a water balloon. The person with the balloon will toss it up and back over his or her head—and the partner will attempt to catch it.

¤ Game Guide

Suggest that all balloons be thrown high. That will give kids more time to attempt to catch them, as well as preventing any direct hits to the back of a partner's head!

Shadow Stomp

Best For: Kindergarten through second grade
Energy Level: High
Supplies: None

The Fun:

Here's a sunny-day game that will produce lots of sunny smiles!

Recruit one volunteer to be your Stomper. Recruit another volunteer to be your Jailbreaker.

Explain that the Stomper will attempt to step on the shadows of other children. The goal of the game is for kids to keep their shadows from being stomped.

If a child's shadow is stomped, that child must freeze until the Jailbreaker stomps on his or her shadow. Then the child can move again.

Be sure to assign a new Stomper and Jailbreaker every few minutes throughout the game.

Echo

Best For: Third through sixth grade
Energy Level: Low
Supplies: None

The Fun:

Echoes are made, not born. Have your kids create their own echoes with this fun, no-prep game.

Form two groups with your students. Ask groups to stand at least ten feet apart, facing each other. Choose one group to begin.

Here's how to play: The child at the end of one line will shout out a word. The other group will loudly repeat the word and the child at the end of that line will add a second word.

The first group will then loudly repeat both words, and the second child in line will add another word. The second group will then repeat all three words and the second child in that line will add a fourth word.

Let the echo continue until one group or the other can't remember all the words and the group flubs the echo.

Words can be Bible verses, random collections, or the world's longest run-on sentence. Just remember, the sequence should always go: add a word and then repeat.

Silly Circles ━━━

Best For: Third through sixth grade
Energy Level: High
Supplies: A plastic baseball bat

The Fun:

Have a ball with a baseball bat—inside!

It's a simple game, but it's lots of fun. Lay a plastic baseball bat on the floor about ten feet from your group of kids. Tell kids that they will run to the baseball bat, one at a time. When they get to the bat, they are to lift the handle so the bat is resting on the floor vertically with the handle up.

Then they'll each place their forehead on the bat and, without lifting the bat from the floor, run around the bat ten times and then dash back to the group. Continue until all children have had a chance to run in this fun relay.

Hug of War

Best For: All ages
Energy Level: Medium
Supplies: One Hula Hoop for every ten kids

The Fun:

Here's a cooperative game that will easily help your kids work together!

Place the Hula Hoops on the floor. Explain to your children that the object of the game is to get as many people as possible standing inside one Hula Hoop. Explain that the game works best if kids follow these guidelines:

● Kids should hang on to each other to keep everyone balanced.

● At least some kids should balance on one foot and hang over the edge of the Hula Hoop.

Let kids play a few rounds of the game to see if they can increase the number that fits into each Hula Hoop.

Human Golf

Best For: All ages
Energy Level: Medium
Supplies: One blindfold for every four kids and carpet squares

The Fun:

This game will help kids have fun together, and will probably bring on lots of laughs.

Have kids form groups of four. Set up a large "golf course" in a park or large playing area, using carpet squares or something similar for golf holes. You'll need at least as many holes as you have foursomes.

¤ Game Guide If you don't have carpet squares, consider using pieces of cardboard, old doormats, or throw rugs. To be fair, just make sure that all of the items you use for holes are of similar size.

Have each foursome begin the game at a different hole. Have groups look at how far it is to the next hole and decide how many normal steps it will take to reach that hole.

Then have each group blindfold one person who will be the Ball, and point him or her toward the hole. That person must walk blindfolded, taking the number of steps the group decided on earlier. Have each group walk with its Ball to keep the person from danger, but group members may not suggest that the Ball alter course (except for the sake of safety) or take a different length of step.

When the Ball has paced off the predetermined number of steps, have the group remove the blindfold to reveal how far the Ball is from the hole. Then have the group determine how many normal steps remain to the hole, choose another group member to be the Ball, and repeat the process until the Ball ends up "in the hole."

A Ball is in the hole only when he or she ends up with at least one foot clearly touching the carpet square. If a Ball crosses over a hole, he or she must keep walking the predetermined number of steps.

As groups complete holes, have them move on to the next hole on the course. Have kids take turns being the Ball. Don't keep count of "strokes," just let kids have fun, no matter how many strokes it takes.

Tunnel Travel ———

Best For: All ages (but best played by kids all around the same age or size)
Energy Level: Medium
Supplies: A watch with a second hand

The Fun:

This game is a tame version of Leap Frog. Instead of going over each other, kids travel under each other!

Have children stand in a line with their hands on the shoulders of the person in front of them. Be sure kids stand with their feet spread apart.

When you give the starting signal, the person at the end of the line kneels down and crawls into the tunnel created by the legs of all the other players. As soon as the first person has begun traveling and has passed through the legs of the person in front of him or her, the second person can begin traveling. Simply put, as soon as you're the last person in line, begin crawling!

This game can be played in two ways. First, kids can race to see how quickly they can get through all players. This means that after each person has gone through the tunnel once, time is called. Kids can race again to improve their time.

A second way to play is for kids to race toward a goal such as a tree, cone, or other object. This means that kids will have to travel through the tunnel two or more times until they reach the goal. Check their time and then have them race back to the beginning in the same manner and see if they can beat their time!

Playground Partners ———

Best For: All ages
Energy Level: High
Supplies: Playground equipment

The Fun:

This partner game helps kids work together in a fun way.

Have kids form pairs and link elbows with their partners. Then explain an obstacle course based on your playground equipment.

For example, you might tell kids to go down the slide once, toss a ball over the monkey bars, go around three times on the merry-go-round, swing twice, then run back to the starting place. The course will depend on what equipment is available on your playground, but try to use as many of the objects as possible. Of course, also consider that two people will be trying to complete this obstacle course together, so don't make it too rough!

If you don't have access to playground equipment, use objects available in your environment, such as trees, bushes, or benches. Just make sure to keep kids away from any traffic dangers.

You can challenge kids in a variety of ways. One way is to time each pair as it goes through the course and then have it try to better its original time.

A second variation is to have all pairs go through the course and time how long it takes everyone to get through. Then have kids change partners and try to better the time.

A final (and a bit confusing) variation is to have all the kids try to complete the course at the same time. Kids can do the obstacles in any order, but they must have a different partner for each obstacle. This means Kenny goes down the slide with Jesse, then Kenny goes on to the swings with Robert while Jesse runs off to the monkey bars to travel on with Mackenzie.

Kids will be dashing madly about trying to find partners and complete the course. This may mean some children will have to go through several obstacles more than once, as they're helping another child complete the course. It's wacky, but it's fun!

Happy Hooping

Best For: All ages
Energy Level: Medium
Supplies: A Hula Hoop

The Fun:

This game poses a problem that can be made easier as group members work together.

Have children form a line, holding hands with those on either side. Give the first child a Hula Hoop. Explain that this child must pass his or her entire body through the hoop, then pass the hoop down the line so it goes over the body of the next person, and so on. What makes this difficult is that the chain of hands must never be broken! It's a challenge for kids to get their bodies through the hoop when they can't let go of those beside them.

Play several times, timing how long it takes for kids to get the hoop from one end of the line to the other. As kids play, they may realize the hoop will move faster as they help each other. They don't have to stay in a straight line, so those with free hands on the ends of the line could help those in the middle. Don't point this out immediately; see if kids can figure out these tricks themselves. The more they help each other, the faster they'll get at passing the hoop!

Thunder and Lightning ━━━

Best For: Third through fifth grade
Energy Level: High
Supplies: Water balloons

The Fun:

This is a great game to play on a hot summer day!
Have all of the children sit in a circle. Ask for a volunteer to be

the Weather Person. Have the Weather Person stand up, and make sure kids leave the space where the Weather Person was sitting.

Give each sitting child a water balloon. Explain that this game is played much like the game Duck, Duck, Goose, except that kids will use water balloons to tag each other.

Instruct the Weather Person to walk around the outside of the circle while gently tapping each child's head or shoulder. Have the Weather Person say "thunder" each time he or she taps a classmate.

When the Weather Person taps someone and says "lightning," the person who was tapped should jump up and try to hit the Weather Person with his or her water balloon.

If the Weather Person sits down in the space he or she vacated before being hit by the water balloon, he or she should be allowed to continue as the Weather Person. If the Weather Person is hit with the water balloon before sitting in the space, the person throwing the water balloon becomes the new Weather Person.

¤ Game Guide

If you want to make certain everyone has a chance to play and you want a defined ending to the game, don't give kids new water balloons after they've thrown them. If you want the game to keep going, give children new water balloons.

¤ Game Guide

If you know you'll be playing this game at your next gathering, you might want to instruct kids to wear old clothing.

Caterpillars ━━━━━

Best For: Kindergarten through second grade
Energy Level: High
Supplies: None

The Fun:

Here's a game that will really get the wiggles out!

Designate an obstacle-free twenty-foot-square area in a grassy field. Choose one child to be the Caterpillar. Have the Caterpillar lie on his or her stomach in the grass. All of the other children should squat next to the Caterpillar and put a finger on the Caterpillar's back.

Then call out, "The Caterpillar's hungry; hop away now!" When you say "now," all the children should hop away like frogs as quickly as possible. The Caterpillar will scurry through the grass on his or her belly and try to tag them. The Caterpillar can also roll to cover ground more quickly.

Any children who are tagged become Caterpillars. When they're tagged, they should fall to the ground and help try to tag the other children. All of the untagged children can hop freely within the boundaries of the playing field.

Play for two minutes or until everyone is tagged. Then choose a new volunteer to be the Caterpillar, and have the kids play again. This time, call out an action other than hopping. Some other actions you might want to try include skipping, walking heel-to-toe, or crab-walking.

An Introduction to Travel Games

"Are we there yet?"

Don't let this plaintive cry resound during your next trip. Use the easy travel games in this section to do more than just pass the time!

Your time with kids is limited. Don't waste precious travel time with kids staring blankly out the window or plugged into their personal stereos. The following travel games are designed to help kids get to know each other better and to help them grow deeper friendships.

Your kids will interact and grow closer as a group, and you'll know you've been a good steward of your time together. And don't worry. All of the games in this section are designed with safety in mind—for both you and your kids! Children should stay buckled up at all times, and the low-energy nature of these games keeps distractions to the driver at a minimum.

And who knows? Maybe kids will be having so much fun along the way, they might actually be sorry to see the trip end!

Jigsaw Stories ———

Best For: Third through sixth grade
Energy Level: Low
Supplies: Slips of paper, pencils, and a bag or a hat

The Fun:

This game will encourage kids' creativity and cultivate any budding authors in the group!

Give each child a slip of paper and a pencil. Instruct each child to write one word on the paper slip. Then have children place their paper slips in a bag or a hat. Mix up the paper slips; then have each child draw a paper slip from the bag.

When each child has drawn a paper slip, designate one child as the Starter. The Starter should begin to tell a story aloud to everyone else, using the word on the paper slip he or she has drawn. When the Starter has presented one sentence of the story, the next child will continue the story, using the word on his or her paper slip in the next sentence of the story. Continue this process until the last child completes the story. Then put the paper slips back into the bag and mix them up. Let children draw out paper slips again, and encourage them to begin a new story. If you choose, use new paper slips for each new story. Choose a new Starter with each new round.

¤ Game Guide
If you have a small group of children, allow each child to tell more than one sentence of the story.

Match It Up! Mix It Up! ———

Best For: Third through sixth grade
Energy Level: Low
Supplies: Index cards, pencils, and two paper lunch sacks

The Fun:

Give each person four index cards and a pencil. Have kids fold each card in half, as if it's a little book. On the first inside page of each "book," have kids write one of the following phrases:

If you have a cold, you should…
When I eat chocolate chip cookies, I like to…
The best way to catch frogs is to…
The key to growing beautiful flowers is to…

Then, on the second inside page opposite the first, have kids complete each phrase. It's important that kids don't share their answers!

When everyone has finished, have kids tear their cards in half to separate the "phrase starters" from the "phrase enders." Place all the phrase starters in one sack and the phrase enders in the other. Have kids take turns drawing one from each bag, and reading the mixed up beginnings and endings. You'll hear statements such as, "When I eat chocolate chip cookies, I like to…go to a muddy place and say 'ribbit.' "

For extra fun, let kids come up with their own phrase starters for the next round of play.

Singing Scrapbook ———

Best For: All ages
Energy Level: Low
Supplies: Paper and a pencil

The Fun:

On a long trip, choose someone to be the Recorder. Give the Recorder a sheet of paper and a pencil; then encourage all travelers to call out names of signs they see. The Recorder will write them down as quickly as possible. Call time after five minutes and have the Recorder read the list aloud. Then have everyone work together to put the list to music.

Choose a simple tune, such as "Happy Birthday to You," "Row, Row, Row Your Boat," or "The Bear Went Over the Mountain." Your song doesn't have to make sense, as long as it includes all the words on the list. The following example of a Singable Scrapbook might be sung to the tune of "Happy Birthday to You."

> Simpson's Auto Repair
> Burger King and Shoe Fair
> Jamie's Flowers, Harkins Theater
> Taco Bell and DQ!

When your song is complete, choose another Recorder, and have the kids play again.

For extra fun, record your songs on a cassette tape. Then you can play back your Singable Scrapbook for a reminder of your travels!

Tell Me More! ━━━━

Best For: Second and third grade
Energy Level: Low
Supplies: None

The Fun:

Have the person whose birthday is the closest to Christmas start the game. Instruct him or her to think of an adjective or "describing" word. Kids might think of sizes, textures, colors, smells, or other descriptive words.

The next person must think of an object with that property and then add another word that would describe the object. Here's the key: Players may not tell what item they're thinking of!

As players add descriptive words, the objects they're picturing will change. For example, if kids have added the words "pink," "living," and "small," the next player might be thinking of a pig and add "noisy." The first person may have had a flower in mind, so when play comes back around, he or she will have to think of a new object that fits all the descriptions.

When a player can't think of an item that might be described that way, he or she says, "Tell me more!" The last person to add a word must tell what object he or she was thinking of.

This is a great game to get kids thinking about the special properties each object has. You may want to talk about God's creativity and God's special love for us.

Story Safari ———

Best For: All ages
Energy Level: Low
Supplies: None

The Fun:

This game exercises kids' creativity while encouraging them to work together to create a fun and unusual story.

Start the game by beginning the telling of an original story. You may want to introduce a few characters, and include a few elements of your own setting, such as items inside your vehicle or at your church. Select a child to take up the telling of the story where you left off. Continue in this manner until each child has had a chance to add to the story.

There are lots of fun variations to make this traditional game unique. Consider these options:

● Indicate the next person to take up the story by including his or her name in the last sentence you add. For example, you might say, "I heard a knock at the door, and when I peeked out the window, I saw Amy standing in the rain." Then Amy begins to add to the story.

● Select a theme for the story. For instance, your story might be a mystery, an animal story, or a rhyming poem.

● Have each child incorporate a number into his or her part of the story. For example, you might begin by mentioning one house; the next person might tell about two dogs; the next person says something about three cars, and so on. For added challenge, tell kids they need to repeat everyone's number phrases already mentioned.

● Use a key word that each person must use in the telling of the story. Choose a silly or hard-to-say word for lots of laughs.

● Have kids incorporate landmarks or the makes and models of passing cars as you drive by them.

Loading Up the Ark ———

Best For: Third through sixth grade
Energy Level: Low
Supplies: None

The Fun:

This game is an excellent way to pass the time on a long trip.

Have kids form two groups. Group members must be sitting in close proximity to one another. Designate one group to be the Bears and the other group to be Lions.

Tell the Bears to think of a category of items. For example, they might think of the category "things you write with." The items in the category could include "pencils," "pens," "crayons," "computers," or "markers." Tell the Bears to make certain the Lions don't overhear the category they choose.

After they choose a category, have one of the Bears reveal an item included in the category by putting it in the sentence, "Noah built an ark, and he put (the item) in it." So if kids chose "things you write with" as a category, the Bear could say, "Noah built an ark, and he put *pens* in it."

Then have a Lion guess the category by repeating the sentence but inserting an item from the category he or she believes the Bears are describing. For example, if the Lion thought the Bears had chosen "things you hold in your hand" as a category, he or she could say, "Noah built an ark, and he put a glass of water in it."

If the Lion's item doesn't fit the category, have another Bear reveal an item in the same way. If the Lion is correct, have him or her guess what category the Bears have chosen. Have the kids continue this process until the category is guessed.

This Old House ——

Best For: Kindergarten through third grade
Energy Level: Low
Supplies: None

The Fun:

This game is an excellent tool for allowing kids to express their creativity.

Tell kids they'll have one minute to tell a story about a building, the people who live in the building or use it, and what happens there. As you drive by a building, say, "(Child's name), who's in that building and what happens in there?"

Give the child one minute to tell others about the building. Encourage kids to be creative with the stories, allowing them to create fantastic situations and characters. Then ask a different child the same question about a different building.

Make certain each child has a chance to tell a story. Don't force any of the kids to tell a story if they don't want to. If kids are timid about speaking aloud or have trouble thinking of what to say, give an example at the beginning of the game by telling your own story about a building. Or, have kids each add a sentence to the story rather than having one child tell about a building. For older kids, allow more time for each of the stories.

Travel Treasure Hunt

Best For: Second through sixth grade
Energy Level: Low
Supplies: Paper and pencils

The Fun:

This game is a great way to get kids to take note of their surroundings while on a trip.

Give each of your students a sheet of paper and a pencil. Give kids a list of ten items they might see while on the trip. Have all the kids write each of the items down on their paper. Include items on the list that you think will be scarce and items that you think will definitely be seen on the trip. You might include some of the following:

- a brown cow
- a cloud shaped like a dinosaur
- a license plate from another state
- a Volkswagen bug
- a car with a cracked windshield
- kids playing games
- a car pulling a boat
- a crow
- a hitchhiker
- a plane
- an amusement park
- a skyscraper
- a bicyclist

- a camper
- road kill
- a shredded tire
- hay
- a shoe
- the McDonald's arches
- someone changing a tire

Adjust the list according to the terrain you expect to encounter. Have all the kids work as a team to complete the list. When someone sees an item on the list, have him or her shout out the item and point to it. Then have all the kids cross the item off their lists. When all the items have been crossed off, give kids a new list of items.

For older kids, use items that are less likely to be seen. For younger children, provide the lists for them by making a handout before the trip. If you have nonreaders in your group, consider using stickers representing common items instead of words.

Time Warp

Best For: Third through sixth grade
Energy Level: Low
Supplies: Watch with second hand or stopwatch

The Fun:

Time flies when you're traveling...or does it? Your kids will find out with this easy game!

Make sure your children can't see a clock. (Confiscate watches and cover any dashboard clock.) Ask two to four children to say "beep" when they believe 107 seconds (one minute and forty-seven seconds) have passed. Explain that kids shouldn't begin marking time until you say "go" and that you should all keep talking as time passes.

As your kids attempt to estimate when time is up, ask direct questions, and keep a conversation going around and—hope-fully—with your kids.

Vary the number of seconds you ask for each time you play the game. Add extra meaning to this game with the following suggestions:

- Sometimes we don't realize how quickly time passes. Ask kids to remember something that happened a long time ago that was so important or fun they can remember it like it happened yesterday.

● Ask kids to think of what is the most important thing they could do with 107 seconds.

● Ask kids what they would do with 107 seconds if that were all the time they had left in life.

Two Out of Three

Best For: Third through sixth grade
Energy Level: Low
Supplies: None

The Fun:

Here's a game that lets children show off what they know!

Explain to children they'll take turns making three general statements, two of which are true and one of which is made up. Tell children to try to make all three statements sound as plausible as possible. Tell children not to make statements about themselves or others in the group.

The rest of your kids will vote on whether the first, second, or third statement is the bogus statement. Then ask the person making the claims to say which two out of three statements are true...and which is false.

Here's an example of what kids might say: Abraham Lincoln was a lawyer before he was president. (True.) The Apostle Luke was a doctor before he was an Apostle. (True.) Jimmy Carter was the governor of Arkansas before becoming president. (False.)

α Game Guide

It's important that all statements be about things another person could have a chance of knowing. "My brother once ate seven hot dogs in one meal" is not exactly a newsworthy announcement! Encourage kids to use biblical, historical, or scientific statements in this game.

Mix 'n' Match ━━━

Best For: First through sixth grade
Energy Level: Low
Supplies: None

The Fun:

Build your kids' verbal skills with this flexible game that's always ready to go!

Tell kids they need to pay special attention to what they see as they look out the car or van window. Challenge your kids to find a "mix" or "match" on a one-mile stretch of road.

A "match" consists of two things they see that start with the same letter or sound. Example: "farm" and "forest" both begin with the letter F.

A "mix" consists of two things they see, with one ending with a certain sound and the other beginning with the same sound. For instance, "pig" ends with the letter G and "garden" begins with the letter G.

Have kids take turns mixing and matching every few miles.

 **αGame Guide**

If you're traveling with fairly young children who are nonreaders or early readers, keep in mind that they can't spell very well—and accept phonetics generously!

Get more mileage out of this game by changing elements of the game every few rounds. Choose from the following game variations.

- Alternate "mix" rounds with "match" rounds.
- Let children work together in pairs or small groups.
- Hold timed rounds (thirty or forty-five seconds).
- Write the letters of the alphabet on pieces of paper and ask children to draw the letters out of a sack. Whatever letter they draw will be the letter they use for their mix or match round.

What Happened to Larry?

Best For: Kindergarten through sixth grade
Energy Level: Low
Supplies: None

The Fun:

Give your kids the chance to find the ultimate hiding place—without ever leaving the car!

Challenge kids to identify places a hypothetical guy named Larry could hide in a game of Hide and Seek. Larry's hiding places must be in the surroundings kids see as they look out the car window.

If you're in the country, Larry might hide in a barn, or behind a tree, or in a cornfield. If you're traveling through a town, Larry might hide in a building or in a parked car.

As you're traveling along, declare that Larry will hide on a designated stretch of road (in rural areas make it no more than half a mile, in the city just a block). Select one volunteer to decide where to hide Larry, and let the other children watch for potential hiding places along the designated stretch of road. Say, "Start Larry's landscape," when you want kids to begin looking for potential hiding places for Larry. Say, "Stop Larry's landscape," when you want kids to stop looking.

After you say, "Stop Larry's landscape," let kids ask the volunteer yes-or-no questions as they try to guess where Larry is hiding. For example, kids might ask the volunteer questions such as: "If it rained, would Larry get wet?" "Can Larry stand up where he's hiding?" or "Will Larry get motor oil on his clothes?"

When kids have guessed Larry's hiding place, choose a new volunteer, and begin the game again.

Sound Bite

Best For: Third through sixth grade
Energy Level: Low
Supplies: None

The Fun:

It's time to use your imagination!

In this game, every player thinks of a famous person and a three- word quote that will help identify the person. The quote can be either a real statement from history, or an imaginary quote that acts as a clue to the person's identity.

For example, maybe the person is a historical personality (Lincoln: "Fourscore and seven..."); a movie character (Arnold Schwarzenegger: "I'll be back!"); or a Bible character (Noah: "On the boat!").

Have kids take turns giving clues as the other kids try to guess the character's identity.

¤ Game Guide

Turn this game into a quick review of Bible characters by asking just for people from the Bible. Examples might include Peter: "I won't deny"; Judas: "Thirty pieces of..."; or Saul: "Persecute the Christians."

As a fun variation, have kids identify the famous person by using three words that suggest the person's identity, rather than using quotes.

For example, Abraham Lincoln might be described with the three words: "Gettysburg," "tall," and "president."

Top Ten Lists

Best For: All ages
Energy Level: Low
Supplies: A peanut, a coin, a stone, and any other object

The Fun:

Affirm your children's creativity with this game—and help make a long trip go a little faster!

Hold up an object—even a familiar one. Ask children to think of ten things they can do with the object.

For instance, a peanut can be a marker in a checker game, shot out of a big straw, crushed to make peanut butter, rolled with your nose in a relay game, and so on. Applaud creativity!

Continue holding up objects. Let children follow the same creative process for each object.

Add extra meaning to this game by asking what children would do with the following objects. Then share with them the stories of how Jesus used the objects.

- a fish (pay taxes; Matthew 17:24-27)
- bread (feed thousands of people; Matthew 14:17-20)

Name That Friend ———

Best For: All ages
Energy Level: Low
Supplies: None

The Fun:

This simple variation of an old rhythm game is an excellent way to help kids learn each other's names. But it can still be a lot of fun even if kids are already friends!

Be sure each child is wearing an easily visible name tag unless all kids know each other's names well. First have each child tell his or her name. Then have kids each find something to safely slap or pat with their hand or fingers. For example, kids might slap their knees or the car seat.

¤Game Guide Remind kids not to disturb the driver by being too loud in this game, or by slapping or patting the back of the driver's seat.

Begin the game by giving kids the following example. Slap something in a regular but fairly slow rhythm five times, saying, "Two, four, six, eight, ten," in the same rhythm. Then mentally choose a child near you, pause for three beats, and continue the same rhythm saying, "(Child's name) is my friend."

After your example, have kids join you in the rhythm and the counting, and say another name. Then have the kids keep up the rhythm and the counting (always saying, "Two, four, six, eight, ten"), and let the person whose name was called say, "(Child's name) is my friend," naming another child present.

No one is to call out a child's name a second time until all kids' names have been called. This game is easily adjusted for younger or older kids by slowing down or speeding up the rhythm. Even with older children, start fairly slowly, and speed up slightly as kids catch on to the game.

Signpost Spelling

Best For: Third through sixth grade
Energy Level: Low
Supplies: None

The Fun:

Make a long trip more fun by passing the time with this fun and easy game.

Before the trip, compile a list of songs your kids enjoy singing. When you're ready to play the game, begin humming the tune to one of the songs until kids can come up with the name of the song.

Don't worry if you're not the world's best singer. Kids will be so busy trying to guess the song, they won't even notice if you're off-key a little!

Then have kids watch for letters on road signs and license plates to spell out the name of the song. Any child may yell out the next letter as he or she sees it. To avoid the embarrassment of someone yelling out the wrong letter, you might want to guide the spelling as it progresses, telling kids the next letter they need to find.

When kids have called out all the letters of the song title, lead children in singing the song through once or twice. Then start humming the tune of another favorite song.

For extra fun, let kids think of and sing the songs. Just make sure they know to choose songs everyone will be familiar with.

α Game Guide

If your kids are too young to spell very well, consider having them find a particular object that represents one of the words in the title. For example, for "Jesus Loves Me," you might have them watch for a cross.

Pass It On ——

Best For: Third through sixth grade
Energy Level: Low
Supplies: Paper, tape, and a Ping-Pong ball (optional)

The Fun:

Passing on the good news about Jesus is the best thing we can do. Children can think about "passing it on" when they play this game.

Distribute paper to each child. Then have each child roll a sheet of paper into a tube lengthwise. Wad a piece of paper into a ball, or use a small ball like a Ping-Pong ball.

Have the first child roll the ball through his or her tube into the tube of the next child. Have that child roll the ball through his or her tube and drop it into the next person's tube. Continue until all children have passed the ball.

There are lots of variations to use with this simple game. Consider these:

● Have kids form pairs, and have pairs connect their smaller tubes. Then let pairs pass the ball to others.

● Send more than one ball through the tubes at a time, staggering the starts. See if one ball can overtake another. You may have to go around the group a number of times to accomplish this.

Take Your Pick ━━━━

Best For: All ages
Energy Level: Low
Supplies: None

The Fun:

This is a fun way to get to know more about the interests of others!

This game can easily be played in pairs, trios, or larger groups, depending on your number of kids. In the game, group members take turns asking each other questions that require the person answering to make a choice. For example, kids might have to decide between...

● ice cream or pizza,
● the beach or Disneyland,
● reading a book or putting together a puzzle,
● playing on the swings or the slide, or
● swimming laps or diving.

You can easily turn this game into a discussion of faith and moral issues by asking other types of questions. For example, kids might have to decide between cheating or flunking a test, or sharing their faith or keeping quiet.

Be sure players have the opportunity to explain why they chose one thing over another. After you've provided a few questions, take turns letting group members think up items, destinations, or activities for others to choose between.

Warning! The older the kids, the more likely this will turn into a "gross out" game. (Would you rather eat worms or termites?) If you see the game heading that way, provide some gentle guidance leading players back toward fun and uplifting choices!

Silly Slogans ━━━

Best For: All ages
Energy Level: Low
Supplies: None

The Fun:

This is a fun game using the numbers and letters from other vehicles' license plates to form silly slogans.

When your car, bus, or van comes upon another vehicle, call out the letters on that vehicle's license plate. For example, if the plate reads, "FWK 225," you'd call out, "FWK." Then kids will quickly take turns making up silly slogans using those three letters, in order, as the first letters of the words in their slogans.

This means FWK could become Four-Wheel King, Fuzzy White Kittens, Frosted White Kookies (you may have to suspend some spelling rules!), or Frank's Wonderful Kangaroos.

Longer sentences can be created from plates with more letters.

Challenge older players by having them use the numbers in the license plates as well.

Beetle Mania ━━━

Best For: All ages
Energy Level: Low
Supplies: Paper and a pencil

The Fun:

This game is great for helping travel time pass quickly!

Determine point values for various types of vehicles or other roadside sights. Let the kids help with this, and write down the point values you decide upon together.

For example, a white car might be worth three points, a "watch for falling rocks" sign could be worth ten points, a billboard for McDonald's might be eight points, and a cow might be worth one point. Assign point values for up to ten different items, remembering to include different makes or colors of cars, specific kinds of trucks, houses, restaurants, road signs, and so on. Keep the point values relatively low, with nothing worth more than ten points.

When the list is complete, begin watching together for the various items, keeping track of the total score as you go. The goal is to get to one hundred points before reaching your destination.

However, if anyone sees a Volkswagen Beetle (or bug, whichever you've grown up calling it), he or she calls out "Beetle Mania!" and all points are erased and play must begin again.

For longer trips, see if you can get to one hundred points before the next rest stop or before a certain mile marker is reached.

After you've reached one hundred points, let kids change the list of what to look for and the items' respective point values. If you like, kids can also choose a new car or other item that erases the points.

People Passing ———

Best For: First through sixth grade
Energy Level: Low
Supplies: None

The Fun:

This is a fun make-up-your-own-story game.

Choose someone in the car to begin the story. Have him or her choose a passing car. The car and its occupants become the beginning facts on which the story is based. For example, the story might be based on an elegant blond woman who drives a fancy gold convertible with a Dalmatian in the back seat. Or the story might begin with two college kids who are wearing tie-dye shirts and are driving a Volkswagen bus with a mural painted on one side.

Have the story starter begin by saying, "Once upon a time there was…" He or she tells the story for a few moments and then points to someone else who will take up where the first person left off. When a new character needs to be introduced, have the storyteller choose another car and weave the car and its occupants into the tale. Play until everyone has a chance to add to the story.

Encourage kids' creativity by asking them to imagine how the occupants in the passing cars are related, where they're going and why, what their jobs are, and even what they ate for breakfast!

An easier variation of this game is to choose a passing car and guess what the driver's life is like based on what you can observe about the car and its occupants. Remind kids to keep their comments kind.

An Eye for Detail ———

Best For: All ages
Energy Level: Low
Supplies: None

The Fun:

This game provides a fun way to develop children's observation skills.

Choose one person in the vehicle to be the Statue. Have the Statue strike a pose while the other people in the vehicle watch. The pose can be serious or silly, complex or simple. Then have all the other children in the vehicle close their eyes while the Statue changes one or more small things about his or her pose. For example, the Statue can close one eye, cross his or her arms the opposite way, or take one shoe off.

When the Statue has changed a small detail, have the other children open their eyes and try to figure out how the Statue's pose has changed. When all of the Statue's pose changes have been guessed, let someone else take a turn as the Statue.

☒ Game Guide Make sure kids playing the Statue remain buckled in their seat belts while striking their poses.

Dark and Stormy Night ▬▬

Best For: Third through sixth grade
Energy Level: Low
Supplies: Paper and a pencil

The Fun:

Tell kids that they are now best-selling authors of mystery or detective stories. Choose a child to start, and hand him or her the paper and pencil. Explain that kids will write a mystery or detective story based on the license plate letters of passing vehicles.

Call out the letters of a passing vehicle's license plate. The child with the paper and pencil will use those letters to create the title of the story. For example, a license plate including the letters GAM could produce a story title such as "Guess Any Murderer."

After the first child has created a story title, have the child pass the paper and pencil to the next child. Call out the letters from another license plate, and have the second child add a sentence to the story. The sentence should include words that begin with those letters from the second license plate.

Continue passing the paper and pencil and calling out letters until each child has had a chance to add a sentence to the story. Then choose a child to read the entire story aloud to the group.

Energy-Level Index

High-Energy Games

Medium-Energy Games

Low-Energy Games